Looking back at
CRAWLEY

Looking back at   *Karen Dunn*
CRAWLEY

with the Crawley Observer and Crawley Times

Crawley Observer   **Crawley Times**

DB PUBLISHING

First published in Great Britain in 2009 by
The Breedon Books Publishing Company Limited
Breedon House, 3 The Parker Centre,
Derby, DE21 4SZ.

This paperback edition published in Great Britain in 2014
by DB Publishing, an imprint of JMD Media Ltd

British Library Cataloguing in Publication Data
A catalogue record for this book is available from the British Library.

ISBN 978-1-78091-400-8

Printed and bound in the UK by Copytech (UK) Ltd Peterborough.

CONTENTS

INTRODUCTION

The best way to learn about a town's history is to ask the people who have lived it – and that is exactly what the *Crawley Observer* has been doing for the past two years.

When the editor pointed to two blank pages on the page plan in 2006 and told me I had to fill them with Crawley nostalgia week after week, my first instinct was to panic and hope that the paper's photograph archives were up to scratch.

I need not have worried. The people of Crawley love their town and the sheer quality and quantity of old photographs that continue to pour into the office never ceases to amaze me.

Particular thanks go to Peter Allen, of Three Bridges, and his never-ending photograph albums; and the team at Crawley Museum, who always do their best to answer questions.

Local historian and teacher, the late Roger Bastable, set the bar remarkably high with his publications on the history of the town that he loved and it is only right to let the people of Crawley tell their tales of school and work, war and peace and relatives long gone who helped make Crawley the fascinating place it is today.

You will read first-hand accounts of doodlebug strikes during World War Two, school life in the 1920s, the bikers of the 1960s who were nowhere near as fearsome as they looked and the Land Girl who refused to give up her job even when the war ended.

Then we have the 96-year-old whose mother took him to school when he was five and then never set foot in the building again; the couple who met hours after a German bomb killed dozens of people and the teacher who stood with a gaggle of excited schoolchildren waiting for the arrival of the People's Princess.

Looking back at *Crawley* has been two years in the making and would not have been possible without the people of this ever-changing town. Thank you all.

Karen Dunn

EDUCATION

There can be few people in Crawley who remember as far back as Stanley Burr. Mr Burr, who turned 96 in 2008, is Crawley born and bred and has clear memories of the tiny village that was destined to become a sprawling new town. Here, Mr Burr recalls his early years and the day he started school.

I started school at the age of five in January 1917. In those days education was a legal requirement for everyone up to the age of 14. The thing that is most in my mind is that at the age of five, my mother took me to school and introduced me to the headmistress, who was a Miss Coward. She then left me. At lunchtime I walked home on my own and returned to school on my own after lunch. My mother never came near the school again.

At that time in Crawley, there were two schools with a playground shared between the two. There was the infants and the primary school which we called 'the Big School'. Teachers I remember from that time are Mr Tongue, Miss Polly Bennett and Miss Holman. Polly Bennett remained a teacher in Crawley for many years and taught not only my wife and me but also, many years later, both our daughters.

The building was divided into three classrooms with a folding partition separating them. With the partitions open it made a big hall, which was used for assembly every morning, but was also used for social events such as concerts. The lavatories were all outside and the pupils had to use them in all weathers, even in the coldest of winters when most of the time they were completely frozen up.

The two schools were known jointly as the Council School and were situated in what later became Robinson Road. There was also a Church of England school called St Margaret's, and this continues to this day on a new site at Ifield.

Robinson Road was named after Sarah Robinson, who lived at the Manor House, which gave its name to Manor Royal. The Manor House stood at the entrance to the estate. She came from a Quaker family who were famous for making Lemon Barley Water and other soft drinks. She was a 19th-century lady and local philanthropist. She was instrumental in setting up both the Crawley Hospital and the first school, known initially as the British School. They came into being through her work, so the name of the road was changed to honour her.

Robinson Road was originally known as Church Lane. In those days it ran from the top of Horsham Road near the current junction with Goffs Park Road, straight down into the town ending at St John's Church. The railway was not there at the time, but it later cut the road in two, and the road was named Post Office Road because it was the site of the Post Office and the Telephone Exchange.

I don't remember much about the actual education, but I do have an abiding memory of the visit of the school dentist. Each term the whole school would have their teeth examined by the school dentist.

I remember having to have a filling. This was done without any anaesthetic and with a drill operated by a treadle and very slow moving. It was the most appalling agony that I can remember.

Another frequent visitor was the nit lady. Most children at the school had head lice, because if one had them, we all had them. I had them from time to time because standards of hygiene were not all that good in those days. The nit lady combed our hair with a very fine comb and it was very painful because children's hair was invariably tangled in those days. Children who had nits were given a letter to take home to their parents, who were advised to wash their hair in carbolic soap.

The school leaving age was 14 and there was no universal secondary education. Most of the children would have gone out to work from the age of 14. The boys would have gone into a trade like building. The largest employer in Crawley was Longleys the builders and the second largest was Cheals Nursery at Lowfield Heath. The girls would either have gone into domestic service or would have worked as shop assistants or seamstresses until they married. It was usual for girls to give up work when they got married, and, in fact, in some jobs girls were forced to leave employment when they married. In particular, girls who worked in the Civil Service and in banks could not continue their employment once they married.

It was possible for a small number of children to gain scholarships to go on to secondary education. These were awarded by the County Council on a means-tested basis.

There was a private commercial school in Crawley where youngsters could go after elementary school to be taught bookkeeping and typing and so on. It was privately owned by a Mr Morris Rushton, who lived in a house called Boscobel House in Crawley High Street.

Council School in the 1920s.    Picture credit: Evelyn Masse

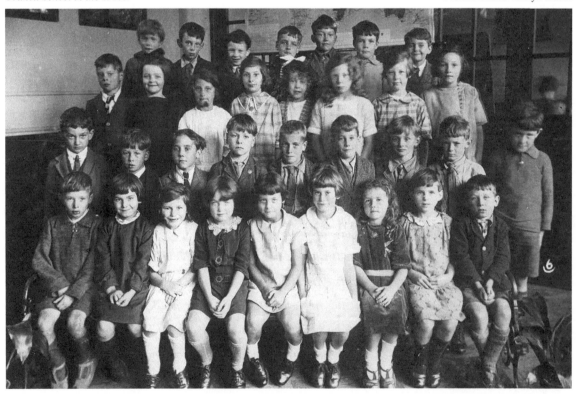

I was fortunate in that my father could just about afford to pay for me to go on to school in Horsham. The school is now called Collyers, but in those days it was known as Horsham Grammar School. It was a fee-paying school and took both day pupils and boarders. We had to go by train on the London Brighton and South Coast Railway, which used to run a special shuttle service between Three Bridges and Horsham. The driver would sit in a cab at either the front or the rear of the train. It was a steam train with two coaches which had a corridor but no doors to the compartments, which were open to the corridor. The train was pulled by Terrier class engines, which, I believe, are still in use on the Bluebell Railway.

When a new boy started at the school we used to get hold of him and put him under the seat on the train. Then we would take the seat cushion off and put it in front of him so that he was trapped under the seat. Then we would all beat the cushions as hard as we could so that all the dirt and dust came out and went all over the poor 'new boy'. If they were wearing a new school uniform it would be completely filthy and as it would have been a major cost to the family this was quite a serious issue.

School uniform was optional and not everyone wore it, but the one thing you did have to wear was a school cap. You had to wear it properly at all times, not only at school but also during the holidays. I still have an old photograph of me with my mother on the beach at Deal in the summer holidays and I still had my school cap on.

At the end of your education you got the Oxford School Certificate, or, if you stayed on, the Higher School Certificate issued by Oxford University. Many employers insisted on it.

I remember, as a child, the great influenza pandemic when millions of people died. There were quite a few people in Crawley who died, including a number of children.

In the period following World War One there was a very deep depression and no state support. It was quite common to see children begging in the streets in Crawley and I can remember seeing children coming to school barefoot in the summer.

One of the best butchers in the town was Horace Yetman who was a pork butcher. His shop was always besieged on Saturday morning by people seeking his pork sausages, which were one-and-three pence a pound. Beef sausages were only eight pence a pound, which meant that you could buy a sausage for a penny and many people used to do that.

In my childhood, most of the road transport was by horses and there were far more horses than cars, which were the exception. There were two blacksmiths and at any time you could smell the burning of horses' hooves.

There were several fishmongers in the town but no refrigerators, although there was a firm from Burgess Hill call Faccenda who used to deliver huge blocks of ice every day. I think they would have been about 1cwt each. The fish was submerged under chunks of ice to keep it fresh. It would have been delivered to Crawley by train from Billingsgate Market and the fishmongers would collect it from the station on little wooden carts.'

EVACUEES

Appearances can be deceptive, and this young group of evacuees were born decades after the end of World War Two. The youngsters were at Three Bridges First School, Gales Place, in 1987, learning about things their grandparents may have experienced.

Leigh White is the fourth little lad from the left and his proud mum Sue said, 'He now is a PC in the London Metropolitan Police working in the Borough of Kensington and Chelsea.'

DINNERLADY

Everyone talks about their favourite teacher – the one who encouraged and nurtured and instilled a love of school into them – but at Three Bridges First School in the 1980s, the school cook was just as important a figure.

Vera Atkinson is pictured serving a tasty meal to a line of children sporting school meal hats. Pat Quaife, of Turners Hill, called her 'our lovely school cook Vera' and remembers her with fondness.

Mrs Quaife was a welfare assistant at Three Bridges School when the photograph was taken in 1988 and has fond memories of appearing in the *Crawley Observer* dressed as 'a naughty schoolgirl minus two front teeth'.

Mrs Quaife worked for West Sussex County Council for 40 years in roles as diverse as lollipop lady, dinner lady and cleaner. She said, 'They say school days are the happiest – they certainly were for me.'

COLLEGE

Ah, college life, there is nothing quite like it. The rag weeks, the tug-o-war contests, the lecturers going on strike – the way the hairstyles of the 1980s dated so badly!

According to the detail on the back of the photograph, these two students were getting ready to take their wall to Paris – though why they were sending a tonne of bricks and mortar to the romantic capital of the world is anyone's guess.

Fashion-wise, it was anything goes in the 80s. Leg warmers and pixie boots were a common sight – and the less said about rara skirts the better – but bin liners?

NATIVITY

Weren't they the cutest little things? These baby-faced angels would have been about five years old when this picture was taken back in 1994, which means they are now adults with more to worry about than who would be Mary and how to make a big white beard stick on a tiny chin.

Former butterfly Harriet Murphy said, 'The nativity scene is from Gossops Green First School. The children in the picture are: Jim Huggins as the lamb, Greg Leneard as Joseph, Megan Broomfield as Mary, Rhian McGovern as the angel, Sally Cooper as the star and I was the butterfly!

'At the time of this play we were in reception and Mrs Bridgeman was our teacher. I can't believe how much everyone has changed and like you said how our priorities change with age and time.

'I seem to concentrate on how I will fit school, homework, friends, going out and working all into one week and back then I really didn't have a care in the world.'

Harriet went on to attend the Holy Trinity School sixth-form with Jim and Megan. She added: 'Rhian left our school to do a sports course at Plumpton College. Greg went to Ifield Community College.'

NETBALL

The following picture of the Crawley Council School girls' school netball team brings back schoolyard memories for Mrs Dorothy Ashfield, of Southgate. Mrs Ashfield, then Dorothy Packham, is pictured holding the ball at the Robinson Road school – where Asda now stands.

She remembers that the teacher's name was Miss Bennett and also recognised Laura Diplock, on the left, Jessie Standen, on the right, and Frida Blundell. She thinks the cookery teacher, Miss Butt, is also in the picture.

Mrs Ashfield was born in Horsham Road in the house opposite the church and loved her time at the school. She said, 'The day I left school I cried, but only because I loved sport.'

She has seen a lot of changes in the area over the years and was able to offer a piece of helpful advice when the road was being redeveloped. She said, 'In those days we had a well in the garden and I have a picture of my mother and I sitting on the well and I am wearing the same clothes. When they were pulling

down the houses I said to one of the workmen "what are you going to do with the well?" He said "there isn't a well" and I said "yes there is". So they covered it. Where I live now the well is in front of my house and that used to be my mum's back yard.'

Gordon Rice's sister Joan (later Joan Woodburn) also attended the school. Joan passed away in 2006, aged 79, within two days of her husband, Woody.

Mr Rice, of Langley Green, said, 'I went there in 1937 at the age of five and left in 1946 at 14. There was a little school Mr Church used to run and then you went into the bigger school. There was a 6ft fence separating the boys' playground from the girls'. Mrs Hogger ran the sweet shop on Robinson Road. We used to go in there for liquorice allsorts.'

Coincidentally, Mr Rice's son worked for the firm that eventually had the job of demolishing the school.

June Read Lorent, from Rockport, Massachusetts, in the US, had many happy memories of her early childhood in Crawley during the 1920s and 30s.

She wrote: 'I was the only member of my family born in Crawley. On 24 June 1927, when I was born, Crawley was a fairly small town. How lucky can one get!

'The West Green school at the infant level was my first experience with learning. Mr Gregory was headmaster and his daughter Margaret also attended. Miss Ansel was standard two and one. Miss Davis, my favourite, was fourth and fifth.

'I loved netball and running. My brother, Ken, was a champion in 100 yards and hurdles. Mr Jones was his teacher at the time.

'To me, it was a very sad day on my 10th birthday when I was told we, as a family, would be moving to Littlehampton. Even today I'm sad when I think of all the happy memories I have of Crawley. But, at the age of 10, one doesn't have a choice.'

ROBINSON ROAD INFANTS' SCHOOL

Arms folded as they gaze solemnly at the camera, this group of little angels could be from any school in Crawley.

The uniforms look much the same as those worn by today's five-year-olds, but this class of scamps attended the Robinson Road Infants' School in 1930.

The picture was donated by Brenda Langridge, of West Green. Then known as Brenda Parsons, she is fifth from the left on the back row. Mrs Langridge has lived in Crawley nearly all her life, having moved to the area in 1928 when she was three. She lived for a while in Three Bridges village. She said, 'At one time they wouldn't let children from Three Bridges go to school in Crawley. We had to go to Worth and it really was awful. I loved it at Robinson Road. Miss Robins was the first-year teacher and Miss Church was the head of the infants' school.'

Children were able to attend Robinson Road from the age of five up to 14.

Mrs Langridge named most of her former classmates. The teacher, Miss Robins, is standing at the back. Back row, left to right: Alan Campbell, Dorothy Sayers, Roland King, Frank Ringrose, Brenda

Picture credit: Brenda Langridge

Parsons, Ronald Etheridge, Richard Miles, Mary Southern, unknown. Second row, from left: unknown, Daphne Surridge, Sam Tidy, Ettie Tullett, Margaret Butcher, Veronica Gelson, Arthur Young, unknown, Walter Chipperfield, Alan Peters, Gladys Emery, Fred Blundell. Third row, from left: unknown, Daphne Williams, Peter Bastable, Stanley Masler. Front row, from left: Maisie Holmes, Frank Jennings, Jean Hounsome, unknown, Joyce Macey, unknown, June Davies, unknown.

ROBINSON ROAD CLASS

This Robinson Road class photograph was taken in around 1950 and the little girl third from the left in the front row is Janet Godsmark.

Picture credit: Marion Godsmark

ST FRANCIS OF ASSISI SCHOOL

This bunch of cheeky chaps were smiling for the camera at St Francis of Assisi School in 1949–50.

Crawley ex-pat Frank Burden, who moved to Courtenay, British Columbia, attended the school 'on its old location now about where McDonalds stands [Haslett Avenue]'. He added, 'I'm in touch with a few of the lads and collectively we have identified just over a quarter of those in the picture. Of course, this is only half of the school population, as there would have been an equal number of girls and three or four nuns.'

Pondering his school days compared to the options available to today's generation of youngsters, Mr Burden said: 'This method of communication is far superior to the old slate and chalk we used at the school in the early days. I well remember sitting on the floor with the little slate board [about 10ins x 12ins] and the stick of chalk practising our letters. I also remember too well the crack across the knuckles we got when we got the letter wrong or broke the chalk.'

Mr Burden stayed in contact with some of his old schoolmates. Michael Goldsmith became a postcard dealer in Twickenham. Alan Bailey moved to Montreal. Terry Mould moved to Oxfordshire. Michael Brackpool retired to Crawley Down. Aubrey Winch moved to Nanaimo, British Columbia. John Fitzpatrick stayed in Crawley. Gerard Jones moved to Devon. Paul Scott became a local politician in Crowborough. Artist Bernard Jones moved to Devon and became well known for his paintings of steam trains. Michael Arnold (absent from the photograph) had a law practice in California.

Mr Burden became a teacher living in Courtenay, British Columbia, on Vancouver Island. He provided a list of names for the boys in the picture. The back row includes: Michael Goldsmith, Colin

Picture credit: Frank Burden

Arnold (deceased), Michael Emery, Dennis Stoner, Neville Hooks, John Benn (deceased), Desmond Dooner, Terry Comper, Bobby Exley. Second row includes: Alan Bailey, Terry Mould, Colin 'Bubs' Stoner, Peter Burden (deceased), Paul Moore (deceased), Ivan des Wart, David Samson, Edward Raines, Michael Brackpool. Third row includes: Gerald Morris, Richard 'Panny' Masters, John Dooner, Aubrey Winch, Teddy Dooner, John Fitzpatrick. Fourth row includes: Derek Edgler, Francis Burden, John Gibb, Brian Whalley, Gerard Jones, Paul 'Snowy' Dooner. Front row includes: Paul Scott, Alfie Manzoli, Raymond Winch, Paddy Dooner, Bernard Jones and Graham Whalley (deceased).

The priest is Father Richard, OFM Cap.

ROBINSON ROAD SCHOOL, 1954

Most of us have looked back and wondered what became of the friends we made at school, but Joan Miller only has to look at this picture of the girls of Robinson Road School, 1954, to roll back the years.

She said, 'I was a pupil at that time and appear in the photograph. Also, there are 14 of us girls in that year who meet up every two months for lunch. Ten of us are in the photograph. The other four must have been away the day the photograph was taken.'

In 2007, the ladies celebrated their 65th birthdays! Joan said, 'After consultation with other members of our group, we have identified all 14 of our group – plus one who lives in San Diego, California, and has attended a couple of our get-togethers.'

The picture above was taken at Christmas 2006 at Goffs Manor and shows (from left, going round the table) Angela Sargeant, Pam Russell, Maureen Douglas, Jean Douglas, Jean Kimber, Kay Donald, Josephine Andrews, Marilyn Weaver, Pat Cooper, Doreen Doughty, Sheila Duffy, Joan Norris, Pam Allen and Yvonne Taylor.

Classmate Christine Harmsworth moved to southern France, but her memories of her time at Robinson Road School in the 1950s stayed strong. Christine sent her best wishes to all her old schoolmates and said, 'I was very quiet and shy so I don't suppose anyone even noticed me, let alone would remember me after more than 50 years!'

SARAH ROBINSON SCHOOL

This group of pictures belongs to Michael Smith, of Northgate, and shows the life and death of Sarah Robinson's school.

The first picture was taken in 1956 when Michael was 14. He is in the second row, fourth from the left. It shows the Robinson Road team which took on Hazelwick in an inter-school sports day. Michael

Picture credit: Michael Smith

cannot recall which school won. He has fond memories of the school, where Mr Keenlyside was the headteacher and Mr Mason taught woodwork. He also remembers Mr Reeson. He said, 'I went to the Church of England school in Ifield Road before I was five. At the age of 11 I went to Robinson Road School. Before I left, I went to the Ifield campus and spent a year at the new Sarah Robinson school at Ifield.

'When I went to the Church of England school, the headteacher was Mr Weston. Mrs Stobbard was the first teacher at that school and she lived in Northgate Road.'

Michael said that the right-hand block of Robinson Road School was for the girls and the left was for the boys.

The last picture shows the final days of the grand old school as it awaited demolition.

ST FRANCIS OF ASSISI SCHOOL, *c*.1948

Most of us look back on our school days fondly and remember them as the best days of our lives, but the old St Francis of Assisi School sounds as if it was something extra special.

This picture belongs to Anita Stone, from Hailsham, and shows her class in around 1948. Mrs Stone remembers the little school as a very happy place. It used to stand where McDonald's is now, on Haslett Avenue, and the children used to trot across to the Friary Hall. Mrs Stone said, 'County Mall used to be our playing fields.' Recalling her time at the school during World War Two, she added, 'It was a very happy childhood. The Canadians used to come in a big lorry and take us up to the huts in Tilgate Park for Christmas parties. They used to give us presents.'

Mrs Stone said Father Ernest was the Friar, while Father Richard was the guardian. She also remembers taking music appreciation with Father Bernadine, who was missing two fingers. She said, 'The nuns were very strict. If you came in without your beret you had to go home and get it. When I think of what they get away with today!

'We used to have lunch at the school – the nuns used to bring it in. We used to have bottles of milk, too. In the winter it was like having a frozen lolly.'

While the school itself holds nothing but happy memories, the uniform was a different matter: 'The uniform was blue. In the summer it was a blue check pinafore – it was horrible.'

Mrs Stone was able to put a few names to faces for the girls' class. The back row includes: Helen Fitzpatrick and Anita Dalby. The fourth row includes: Kathleen Smith, Mary Rice, Barbara Meeton, Patsy (?), Betty Morris (deceased), Kitty Smart, Sheila Muggridge, Mary Parker, Kathleen Smart, Sylvia (?). The third row includes: Diane Parker, Patsy Morris, Stella Rice and Myrtle Whalley. The second row includes Ann Bass, and the front row includes Angela Benn and Ann Rice.

THE MILL PRIMARY SCHOOL

Lined up for the camera, their uniforms neat, their expressions serious, these two groups of children look similar. But the little 'time travellers' below are separated by a century from the children above. Their uniforms have changed and their toys are a world apart – and the idea of keeping boys and girls separated must seem very strange to the Crawley kids of today.

With Crawley, Ifield and Three Bridges still separate villages, the Edwardian children would likely be overwhelmed by the sheer size of the new town. And how would today's youngsters cope without family cars, computers and televisions?

As part of their celebration of Crawley's 60th birthday in 2007, this group of five-to-nine-year-olds from The Mill Primary School followed in the footsteps of their ancestors and headed off to Ifield Mill, the church and, finally, the site of the original Ifield School.

Headteacher Roz Smart said, 'Apple Class and Silver Birch Class set off to Rusper Road, armed with a fantastic old Edwardian photograph we had found tucked away in our resources room. The children then did their best to recreate the pose of those children nearly 100 years ago, including boys and girls strictly segregated!'

Picture credit: The Mill Primary School

Colin Edgar, of Southgate, added, 'The photograph was taken in about 1903. I can pinpoint this date as my granddad, Raymond Chantler, is not in it and he attended the school from 1903.

'Looking at the picture of the teacher, a Mr Jutson, and looking at him in a picture with my great aunt in 1907 he looks younger. The school tower still remains on the site. The school was hit by a flying bomb in 1943, never to reopen. The children then attended the school at Little Deerswood. The building was to the right of the Masonic Temple. I went there from 1953–55 until they finished building Ifield Junior School opposite and St Margaret's School in the Mardens. Pupils from here and the Crawley school then filled the spaces.'

ROBINSON ROAD SCHOOL FOOTBALL TEAM

This line-up of sporty lads played for Robinson Road School football team in 1946–47. The picture belongs to Sheila White, of Langley Green.

Picture credit: Sheila White

ROBINSON ROAD SCHOOL IN 1955

They say your school days are the best of your life, and the lads and lasses above certainly seem to be enjoying themselves. The following picture was taken at Robinson Road School in 1955 and belongs to Sheila Fox.

Mum-of-two Sheila, who lives in Furnace Green with her husband Barry, said 'Each class had its own Christmas party and this was ours. I think our teacher was Mr Reeson at that time.'

Of her former classmates, Sheila named Joan Norris, Josephine Andrews, Kay Donald, Jean Kimber, Maureen Douglas, Jean Douglas, Diane Harland, Gloria Maynard (deceased), Terry Chance, Geoffrey Butcher, George Martin, Ann Simmonds (deceased) and Christine Taylor. She said, 'I'm there of course and was Sheila Duffy in those days. I'm sure there are others I could identify but those are all I can remember at the moment.

'When I left school I went to Crawley College and trained as a secretary – a decent job in those days as only senior directors had secretaries, everyone else used the typing pool. We learned elocution and

Picture credit: Sheila Fox

deportment, how to get in and out of a car, which drinks went in which glasses, how much to pour into each glass, amd how to address titled people and senior members of the clergy. Perhaps they thought we would meet these people in our careers. Of course, we learned shorthand and typing. Nobody would be employed as a secretary without being proficient at both.'

THOMAS BENNETT COMPREHENSIVE 1ST XI

These fresh-faced lads made up the Thomas Bennett Comprehensive 1st XI of 1960–61, and the picture belongs to Ken Bateman, who emigrated to New Zealand in the 1980s. Ken named the players. Back row, left to right: Paul Talbot, Nick Frosthaus, Alan Henderson, Ken Bateman, Phil Keenlyside, Mick Bell, Tom Plimmer, Ian Jones. Front row: Greg Strange, Jimmy Knox, Terry Wheeler, Pete Butler and Pete Higgins.

He added, 'Paul Talbot lived around the Tunbridge Wells, Uckfield area, married and ran his own garage. Mick Bell worked on the Petticoat Lane market before emigrating to Australia. Greg Strange moved to Aberdeen and became a quantity surveyor and a world-famous mountaineer. Jimmy Knox, the best footballer by far of the team, trialled for a professional team. Unfortunately he died. Terry Wheeler trained at Brighton College of Education as a PE teacher. Pete Higgins became a well-respected architect in London.'

Ken lived at Stonefield Close until 1967 before going to Brighton Polytechnic for a mechanical engineering degree. He worked at APV then travelled around New Zealand, Australia and the Far East before returning to the UK. He played rugby for St Francis, Crawley, from 1974 to 1985 and worked at Nestlé in Croydon from 1976 to 1985.

Picture credit: Ken Bateman

He married Jacqui and emigrated to New Zealand in 1985. He has been living in Palmerston North for 18 years and working for a local engineering company.

Ken says he is almost a Kiwi and supports the All Blacks – but not for the World Cup, when his loyalties lie with England!

THOMAS BENNETT COMPREHENSIVE

Boys will be boys, and this bunch of likely lads got a taste of the lighter side of school by larking around behind the bike sheds at Thomas Bennett. The picture belongs to Robert Collins, of Copthorne.

Picture credit: Robert Collins

THREE BRIDGES JUNIOR SCHOOL *c.*1947

These boys and girls do not look too happy to be in lessons. The picture belongs to Pete Allen, of Three Bridges, and shows one of the classes at Three Bridges Junior School in around 1947.

Picture credit: Peter Allen

THREE BRIDGES JUNIOR SCHOOL SPORTS DAY, *c.*1948

Picture credit: Peter Allen

POUND HILL JUNIOR SCHOOL

Whether your school days were the best of your life or you couldn't wait to get out, you cannot help but look back at old class photographs and smile.

This picture belongs to Allan Bailey, of Bewbush, and shows his classes at Pound Hill Junior School. It was taken at Pound Hill in around 1958 and the teacher's name was Miss Berry. Of his former classmates, Allan was able to name Sandra Gladwin, Robert Collins, Nicky Froshough and Graham Letchford.

Picture credit: Allan Bailey

HAZELWICK, 1962

This picture was taken at Hazelwick in 1962.

Picture credit: Allan Bailey

HAZELWICK ATHLETICS TEAM, 1962

Here we have the Hazelwick Athletics team of 1962. Former pupil Allan Bailey said, 'We always used to beat Thomas Bennett!'

Picture credit: Allan Bailey

Allan named: Peter Love, Roger Brazier, Dave Vallance, Peter Silk and William Howick, Barry Concanon, Susan Thomas, Jane Gray and Robert Batey.

ST WILFRID'S SCHOOL

2008 saw the end of an era for St Wilfrid's School, in Southgate. Despite the building being damaged by fire, the new school was well on target for its grand opening in February 2009.

St Wilfrid's School was founded in 1953, located in a building called

Picture credit: St Wilfrid's School

Oakwood on the south-west side of Crawley, which now forms the administration block. Oakwood was previously a private residence with an interesting history.

The house was built in 1872 for General Charles Longden, who had recently retired from the Royal Artillery having served in China and India in the Indian Mutiny. He bought the land (nine acres) and built a smaller house than the one we see today on what was called Perry Field. He died in 1894, aged 72, and the property was passed to his son the Revd Henry Isham, a clergyman in the Anglican Church, but due to Henry's duties for the church he did not live in the property.

It was then sold to Philip Saillard, a merchant for ostrich feathers, but he, again, did not live in the house, instead seeing it as an investment. The house was then sold to a Horace Hill, who worked as a printer in London.

The Hills found the house too small and embarked on a building programme, which included work on the front of the house to give the façade that was to become familiar to generations of schoolchildren.

The association with schools started at that time as Mrs Hill generously let Crawley schools use the grounds for an inter-schools sports meeting in 1933. The Hills sold the house in the same year to Mr Shirley Hall Birt, who was a retired doctor from the Navy. He died in 1938 and his estate sold the house to Antonio Gordon, whose family came to England and set up a wine importing company with the sole agency for importing Domecq Sherry.

The house and grounds were later offered to the Catholic Church, who saw the need for a secondary school in the area to offer a good all-round Christian education and purchased the property for the sum of £12,500.

St Wilfrid's Catholic School opened its doors in September 1953.

Picture credit: St Wilfrid's School

The picture was taken in 1954 and shows the first prefects and staff to attend St Wilfrid's. Back row, left to right: P. Pannell, G. Martin, E. Ward, B. Green, F. Lee, J. Vigar, T. Lambert, J. Butler-Browne. Front row: Mr D. Grindlay, Mr T.G. Jackson, Miss P. Fullaway, Mr M. O'Reilly (headmaster), Miss B. West, Mr R. Hemming, Mr D. O'Connor.

NORTHGATE SCHOOL AND WORTH SCHOOL, 1954–55

Years may pass and times may change, but there is one constant when it comes to the minds of school kids – football is much more important than lessons!

These little tykes smiling for the camera were the 1954–55 players for Northgate School and Worth School in the Crawley Junior School League. The picture belongs to John Skinner, now of Suffolk, who played at right-half (defender) for Northgate. Mr Skinner said, 'In those days we had to walk all the way from Northgate to the Old Worth School, which was on the Turners Hill Road, which was some walk before playing a football match – and back to Northgate afterwards!'

Worth won the match 3–0 and Onlooker from the *Crawley Courier* was very impressed by what he saw, penning an enthusiastic report for the paper. Under the headline 'Soccer with spirit' he wrote: 'Picture the scene. Twenty-two mustard-keen schoolboys haring after a football, spurred on by the urgent howls of their class chums and the promise of a ticking-off by their sports master coaches, who probably lose more sleep over their teams' efforts than Arsenal chief Tom Whittaker does over Danny

Picture credit: John Skinner

Blanchflower, and you can conjure up some idea of the spirit that goes into Crawley Junior School League matches.

'School football in Crawley is nothing new but I must confess that this is the first time I've had the opportunity or to be more honest, taken the trouble to drop in at a local schoolboy match.

'A pleasant surprise awaited me at Worth last Thursday. School football, believe me, is no joke. These tearaway youngsters (average age 10) may be pint-sized but they have the grit and determination of many an older player.

'Mr Eric Thomson, Northgate's sports chief, told me that every one of his lads takes his game seriously, and judging by this hectic ding-dong struggle, Worth don't treat school football as a holiday.

'Worth are undoubtedly an outstanding team. Previous to this game they had scored 23 goals without reply from their opponents and despite the tenacious energies of the red-and-white-shirted Northgate boys they retained their unbeaten (no goals against) record. They fielded three reserves for this game but the changes didn't weaken them for they possess more than one player of rare calibre for his age.

'Their forward line harbours the stars, with diminutive Charlie Casselden rating a shade above his colleagues, Ted Heaysman and Robert Hazlewood, who are both prolific goalscorers. Outstanding in the Worth defence was David Gardner, a steady little left-half.

'Northgate were expected to and did give Worth their toughest game so far. With a few more breaks they might even have won the match. Both their full-backs, Hunter Jarvie and Robert Weaver, covered goalkeeper Triggs well, and ginger-headed John Skinner at right-half was one of the best players on the field.

'Play throughout maintained a pace far above what I had expected and there was no second half flagging. After Hazlewood – he has scored eight this season – had narrowly failed to net, Heaysman put Worth ahead with a fine dropping shot from the right wing. Terence Warwick added a second almost immediately when goalkeeper Triggs made his only mistake of the game. Heaysman scored the only goal of the second half and Michael Little hit the bar for Northgate.

'Finally, a word of praise for the Worth official who refereed superbly. Ignoring all but the most obvious of offsides and foul throws, he continually shouted words of encouragement and advice to both teams. All strictly against the rules but none-the-less words of wisdom to these eager midgets.

'Footnote: Watching the game during the first half was Mr J. Boyce, deputy director of education for West Sussex.'

Referees ignoring offsides and no one complaining about it? Players being called eager midgets? Times have certainly changed!

The team line-up is (back row, left to right): Laurie Simpson, Robert Weaver, David Hall, Bernard Triggs, Hunter Jarvie, John Skinner, David Gardner, Jimmy Wake, David Sayers, Barry Cheesmur, John Bryan, Paul Lyndon. Front row: Barry Phillips, Stanley Trevaskiss, Michael Little, Terry Sales, Nigel Unwin, Terence Warwick, Richard Hounsome, Robert Hazlewood, Charlie Casselden, Ted Heaysman.

LEISURE

4TH WORTH SCOUTS, 1913

These young Scouts were lined up for a celebratory photograph to mark their pack's fifth anniversary. The picture shows the boys of the 4th Worth Scouts and was taken in 1913.

The late Jean Steele, former chairman of the group, said 'I think the picture may have been taken at the home of the Misses Nix, in Worth, which is where the boys used to meet.'

The group celebrated its centenary in 2008.

CRAWLEY CARNIVAL 1987–89

Time to take a leap back to the days when Crawley Carnival boasted a colourful procession which set off from the car park opposite the railway station – where the County Mall shopping centre now stands.

These pictures were taken at the carnival between 1987 and 1989.

CRAWLEY CARNIVAL QUEENS

This bevy of beauties from decades long gone are Crawley Carnival Queens – and young women who competed for the crown – from as far back as the 1940s and as 'recently' as the 1970s.

Hayley Thorne wrote about one of the Carnival Queen contenders – who went on to become her grandmother.

Mrs Thorne said, 'In the photograph (below) of the five girls who have hats on and are sitting on a truck – my grandmother is the one standing up. Her name at the time was Daphne George. I have this photograph at home. Also, she is in the line up of the five girls – she is holding the number 21. It looks to me that the five girls in the line up are the same as those in the hats and sitting on the truck.'

Daphne died in January 2004.

CARNIVAL PRINCESSES

Back in the eclectic 80s with another bunch of Carnival Queens and Princesses – and these little ladies seem delighted to have been chosen to be Carnival Princesses.

Chivalry was alive and well in the 80s as our picture shows. It may have been muddy and a bit chilly, but one Sir Walter Raleigh wannabe was quick to lay his T-shirt on the boggy ground to stop the 1985 Carnival Queen getting her feet dirty.

A girl never forgets when she competed to be Carnival Queen for a day. Beverly Guy, now Beverly Daniels, came second in the 1975 contest to find the queen and her attendants. She said, 'The contest was held in a local airport hotel. It was a very exciting experience, I was 17 and studying for my A levels at Thomas Bennett Comprehensive School. I had a great year, working with the wonderful Crawley Lions – a busy time doing publicity and charity events, and much fundraising.

'I still have the beautiful blue dress I wore on the carnival day and the pink sash too!

'Thanks to the Lions Carnival Queen contest, I met my husband while on a fundraising engagement. Funny old world isn't it!'

Beverly moved to Worthing with her husband and two sons. She taught music in a local independent school and in her spare time enjoyed treading the boards, singing and dancing in musicals at Worthing's Connaught theatre. She added, 'The Carnival Queen, Sandra Ives as she was then, was an air hostess and I have often wondered what happened to her. The other contestant was named Angela. Sorry, I don't remember her surname. We had a lot of news coverage in 1975. The carnival was a very big event in the community in those days.

'Our 1975 carnival day was particularly memorable because it was nearly ruined by a drunken lad chucking a bucket of water over Sandra while we were walking around the carnival field. We made the headlines for all the wrong reasons!'

It has been a few years since Sandy Ives lined up for a picture of the 1975 Carnival Queen and her attendants, but she is living life to the full. Sandy travelled a lot, both working and living abroad. In 1992 she set up home in Brittany, France, with her partner and three children. She said, 'We live on a peninsula, one side is the Golfe du Morbihan with its many islands which you can visit, and on the other the sea. Only 20 minutes from here is the medieval town of Vannes. I teach English. My partner is also a teacher and author of school material, children's novelist and journalist. That is why we both became involved in writing school documents to try to make life a little more interesting for children.

'Due to the fact I spoke very little French when I arrived (as I had been living in a Spanish-speaking country before) I couldn't find a job. France didn't accept "foreign" diplomas. Even with Europe today it's not always easy for outsiders to find jobs here in France. So I decided to start teaching English.

'The school where my daughter was asked me to teach the 9–10 year olds. Soon other schools heard about me and I found I was getting more and more offers.'

Sandy soon qualified as a teacher for primary schools. She said, 'At that time English wasn't part of the school curriculum.'

CRAWLEY CARNIVAL IN 1984

No matter how chilly it is outside, there is nothing like a few carnival pictures to remind us that the sunny weather is on the way. This collection of photographs was snapped at the Crawley Carnival in 1984.

The finalists in the Carnival Princess competition are lined up opposite, while 'Charlie Chaplin' doffs his bowler hat. Sandie Sexton, of Maidenbower, wrote of 'Charlie': 'He was my husband Mike's uncle, Jim Clinch. Jim was well known in Crawley and always dressed as Chaplin to raise money for charity, his main one being Dogs for the Blind; although he also collected for Cancer Research, which would make the family laugh as he was a 40-a-day man!'

'He and my husband's aunt lived at Rusper after marrying, along with my husband's parents and their four children. They never had children of their own. He worked for many years at Langley London in the warehouse, sweeping and tidying up.

'He was well known in the Crawley and Horsham area. He sadly passed away 10 years ago but the whole family are pleased to know he was remembered in this way.'

WEST GREEN DRIVE PLAYGROUND

We have all heard it from our parents and grandparents: 'Kids have never had it so good', they declare, 'In my day we had to make do with a hoop and a stick…' and so on. A slight exaggeration, perhaps, but compared with the youngsters who were growing up when the new town was young, today's children have a plethora of places to go to keep them amused.

This picture belongs to Rae Carman and shows Crawley's first adventure playground being built in West Green Drive, although she is not sure of the date.

FAMILY FESTIVAL OF 1987

Crawley has always known how to throw a party and the people in these pictures from the Family Festival of 1987 certainly seemed to be having a good time.

It was the year Terry Waite was kidnapped in Beirut and 31 people perished in the King's Cross tube station fire; Nirvana formed and The Smiths called it a day.

It is every 10-year-old lad's nightmare. You are snapped by a photographer for the local paper – a picture all your mates are going to see – and you are sitting next to your mum!

Simon Brobyn, of West Green, is sitting on this trailer being pulled by a traction engine in Goffs Park in the 1980s. Simon, who went on to work for Blue Inc., was taken along to the August bank holiday fun day by his mum, Jenny. Simon is now a dad himself and dotes on his daughters Jolie and Callie.

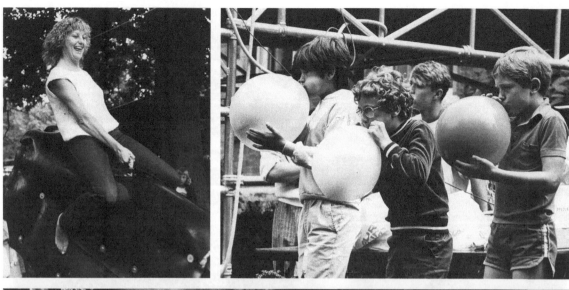

Mr Albert Urben organised the vintage vehicles that made the day such a success and said the traction engine driver was Mr Hayne, who lived in Pulborough. He remembered the events as 'absolutely brilliant' and had fond memories of the funfair organised by Dougie Harris. He said, 'It was like a family get-together. It was a shame it fell through.'

1992 CARNIVAL

The sun was shining for the 1992 carnival – and a fun day was had by all.

The little architect and builder were Tom and Elli Riddick. Their mum Sue Wickstead said, 'Ahh! Yes, I remember it well. At the time I was the co-ordinator of the Bewbush Playbus. We were attending

the Crawley carnival as usual and my two children were dragged along. Tom was the architect and Elli the builder. We always tried to decorate the playbus as best we could to match the theme of the carnival. I think we won overall cup for the bus and Tom and Elli won a prize for their fancy dress.'

The brother and sister went on to separate universities with Tom attending Winchester while Elli studied at Southampton.

SPRING FAIR, 1991

The Spring Fair of 1991 had more than its fair share of sunshine and the little lad pictured right tried to cool down with an ice cream.

Being just a wee chap, he ended up with more of the treat on his face than in his mouth!

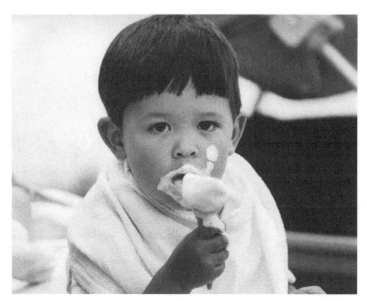

CRAWLEY TOWN BAND

Crawley has been home to a wide variety of music over the years, from the New City Jazzmen to the legendary Cure, but the men in these pictures were around decades before Robert Smith learned his middle C from his B flat.

This picture shows the Crawley Town Band of 1902.

This one is labelled as the Crawley Town Prize Band of 1906.

The next picture is unlabelled and undated.

This picture is dated 1913 and shows the Crawley Town Band, winners of the Southern Counties Championship.

CRAWLEY TOWN MILITARY BAND FROM 1935

This picture shows the Crawley Town Military Band from 1935. It is dated 10 June and declares the band to be winners of the Southern Counties Band Association Military Band Contest.

The band had taken part in a contest at the Recreational Ground, adjudicated by Dr Denis Wright. Only two other bands, Reading Temperance and the Horsham Town Band, took part in the military band section. All the other sections were for brass bands only.

All three were required to play a test piece – *Carmen*, by Georges Bizet – and a march of their choice. Crawley played Kenneth Alford's *On The Quarter Deck* and won the contest.

The boy second from the right, seated at the front and clutching a clarinet, is Bob Sorrell. Bob married Sheila and the couple set up home in Haywards Heath.

The other bandsmen included: Back row, from left: Bill Reid, Laddie Parker, S. Knight, Bill Barman, Clar Parsons, Bert Austen, (two unknown), Bill Pullen, Claude Smith, Frank Ford. Middle row, from left: Mr Lee, Harry Bacon Snr, Geoff Comfort, George Bulman (?), Claude Bowers, Charlie Martin, Wilf Charman, Bob Couchman, Stan Earl, George Beal. Bottom row, from left: Ernie Freeman, George Parker, Mr Martin, Mr Smith, John Penfold, Albert Heather, Walter Ellis, Captain Smith, Albert Branston, Bill Pellen, Bill Robinson. Boys, from left: Harry Bacon, Bill Tappenden, Bob Sorrell, Denis Tullet.

Dennis Finch, of Three Bridges, had two uncles who played the cornet in the Crawley Silver Band. They were called Bert and Charlie Brown. Charlie, the younger brother, was born in 1890 and was 40 years to the day older than Dennis.

Bert lived in Ifield Wood and was bailiff for a millionaire who lived in Ifield. Charlie lived on Horsham Road and went on to be a caretaker in St Giles School, Croydon, in the 1930s and 40s. The school catered for disabled children and Charlie's wife, Annie, was the cook.

Mr Finch recalled that Bert married Annie's sister Louis and they had a son and daughter, though Charlie and Annie had no children.

Mr Finch said, 'People used to call Bert "Buster". I can only remember meeting him once. We used to visit Charlie at the school so I knew him quite well. He and Annie moved back to Horsham Road after they retired.'

When the call to fight for King and country was put out, many of Crawley's heroic young bandsmen were among those who laid down their lives. Amateur historian Russell Gore said, 'There is a town band memorial plaque in the church of St John's in Crawley town centre. On the plaque are the names of eight men of the band who died during World War One. Another picture of a town band is on display in the Plough public house in Three Bridges and this picture is of the Crawley Temperance League Town Band. It seems ironic that this photograph is now on display in a pub!'

The details of three of the men are:

D. Duffell, driver, Army Service Corps, 29th Div. Train. Died on 4 September 1915, aged 20. Service No: T/35424. He was the son of George and Emily Duffell, of Chapel Lane, Charlwood, Horley. His grave can be found at the Alexandria (Chatby) Military and War Memorial Cemetery. Charles Alfred James Rice, Serjeant, The Buffs (East Kent Regiment), 1st Battalion. Died on 29 January 1919, aged 27. Service No: L/9464. He was the son of James and Ann Hannah Rice, of Malthouse Road, Crawley; husband of Nellie Rice, of 13, Malthouse Road, Crawley. His grave can be found at the Terlincthun British Cemetery, Wimille.

William Henry Clark (listed as Clarke in some places). Rifleman S/5620, 10th Battalion, Rifle Brigade. 20th Division. Killed in action on the Somme 3 September 1916. Born in Buckswood, Ifield, and enlisted in Holborn. Next of kin Balham, South London. Clarinet player in Crawley Town Band. Father William Clark from Handcross. Commemorated on Thiepval Memorial, Somme, France.

THE BEWBUSH PLAYBUS

Children who grew up in the 1980s and 90s will recognise the Playbus straight away, and it was a familiar fixture at the Dorsten Square car park in Bewbush.

It all began when the south-east branch of the Girl Guides Association chose to spend their portion of the Queen's Silver Jubilee Fund on a project in the new neighbourhood of Bewbush. At the time Bewbush had no community centre, and a community bus seemed to be an ideal temporary solution. After it had been converted and painted by BAA and BCal, Lady Baden Powell officially presented the bus – then called Supersonic – to Bewbush in August 1980, and it was put to use in a summer playscheme and then as a pre-school playgroup.

And its 'temporary' status ran on and on and on...

Sue Wickstead, of Furnace Green, played a huge part in making the bus the success story it became. She said, 'I came to Bewbush in about 1985 and I looked around for playgroups. A friend suggested the

Playbus. The bus had seen better days. They had sold the space on the side of the bus to a carpet shop and they had splashed a huge advert across it – it looked awful.'

Not content to simply be one of the parents, Sue threw herself into improving the bus – and the first thing it needed was a paint job. With the help of Gatwick Engineering and an awful lot of paint, the new nursery rhyme design took shape – though the children soon noticed that Humpty Dumpty was very naughty as he was looking straight into the toilet window!

The Playbus hit a new high when it took the lead in the carnival procession of 1987, but a low followed when it was vandalised – a distressing trend that was

to plague the scheme year after year and resulted in one of the buses being scrapped in 1991.

Sue, who became a primary school teacher, discussed her time with the bus with enthusiasm, speaking highly of the people involved over the years – names like Trevor Bastin and Angela Flatt – without whom it would never have been such a success. She said, 'The first driver was Phil Avery and the children loved him. He used to drive the bus to Gatwick for safe keeping.'

The bus spent a lot of time at the airport after being invited to entertain bored children when the airlines were choked by delays. Sue said, 'We parked outside the North Terminal and it was so well received. We had grandparents who came along and played with the Lego.'

The 1990s were exciting times for the Playbus team. News reached them that there was a national

Playbus organisation – they were not alone – and the old bus made trips to Newcastle and back to take part in bus rallies. And in 1992, when the Worthing scheme folded, Sue signed a deal with them to buy their red 1968 Leyland Atlantean NRG 176M for the grand price of £5. 'The Bewbush bus was the first of many in Sussex. We were a pioneering group. I enjoy teaching and I like to think I'm a better teacher because of the Playbus.'

PHIL AVERY

Phil Avery, the first Playbus co-ordinator/driver, said, 'I have the fondest memories of 14 years of my life spent on this pioneering project. Bewbush at the time [1980] was a brand new estate, with many young families but few community facilities. Children under five years were soon identified as being in great need of playgroup facilities.

'In the absence of suitable buildings for the purpose, the notion of a mobile base was suggested, and through the combined efforts of a team of totally dedicated people the Bewbush playbus was born.

'I recall the following personnel as being the ground workers of the project. The lynchpin was June Spaull of Crawley Social Services Dept [the then under-fives' advisor for Crawley]. June was the first to get the ball (or should I say "the bus") rolling. A phone call from the Girl Guides Association was received at Social Services offering funding for a community project, and from that moment the wheels were turning.

'Dave and Vic Hastings were members of the steering committee along with others (whose names escape me at the moment). A suitable bus was purchased from Eastbourne Bus Company and expertly converted by the apprentices of British Caledonian Airways.

'Playgroups were now ready to open. The first supervisors were Barbara Conley, Sue Boxall and Lyn Constable, ably assisted by Angela Flatt and a small band of volunteers. During my involvement with the Playbus, a steep learning curve presented itself. Driving lessons from Syd Peters (Thanks again, Syd) and tuition on starting portable generators, firing up the central heating and servicing chemical toilets, all had to be mastered. I would guess that around 150 children used the Playbus during my time there, 1980 to 1994, and I'm sure that they all enjoyed a unique playgroup experience.

'To say that you never know quite what will happen when you join a new project is for me a huge understatement. How could I ever have known that I would meet my lovely wife Val on a double-decker bus (Val was the afternoon playgroup supervisor). Quite remarkable!

'Our wedding day was made complete by the appearance of the Playbus outside the church, and we rode as passengers to our reception. We found two bottles of champagne in the sand tray, which made the journey all the more enjoyable. To this day we don't know who put them there. Years on we are still happily married and now provide foster care for special needs children.

'Working with such a good team of staff and volunteers was wonderful, and the experience of meeting and working with so many Bewbush families and sharing their lives was a real privilege for me. May I take this opportunity to say "hello" and a big "thank you" to everyone I knew connected with the Playbus, and congratulate everyone concerned for keeping the project running for so long.'

THE PLAYBUS IN THE 1980S AND 90S

Smiling for the camera in these pictures are some of the young lads and lasses who passed many a happy hour in the Playbus in the 1980s and 90s.

The group shots show children from 1983 and 1985, while the lads and lasses from the Playbus after-school club of 1990 were enjoying an Indian powwow one sunny afternoon in July.

CRAWLEY OPERATIC SOCIETY

Since 1957, Crawley Operatic Society has been entertaining audiences with their take on some of the greatest plays of all time – and society member Charlotte Cosh, from Southgate, knows exactly who should take a lot of the credit. She said 'We have to thank Carl Willmott, the first headmaster of Sarah Robinson Secondary School, in Ifield, for getting the entertainment started. It was not long after the school came into use in 1956 that Carl produced *Trial by Jury* with pupils as the chorus and teachers as the leads. This was such a success that Carl decided to investigate the possibility of staging further concerts, and to this end he invited a cross section of people he thought would be interested. His idea

Picture credit: Crawley Operatic Society

Picture credit: Crawley Operatic Society

was to form a group of people to put on future shows, and from the outcome of a gathering on 27 April 1957, the Sarah Robinson Group was born.

'The Evening Institute at Sarah Robinson was also new and the county council very readily agreed to accommodate the group as an Evening Institute class, with members meeting on a Monday evening. This has never changed over the past 50 years, with company rehearsals taking place on Monday.

'The Sarah Robinson Group's first production was *HMS Pinafore*, scheduled to take place for three nights in November 1957. Production was put together after fundraising at the Crawley Carnival and a grant of £5 from some obscure source. This, however, had to be rescheduled due to the musical director being taken ill, to January 1958. Even then things did not go smoothly; the show was short of men, so ladies were persuaded to take the part of sailors.

'Despite these setbacks, the show was a great success and was financially successful, with production costs of £120 and ticket receipts of £145. This is in stark contrast to production costs today, in excess of £28,000 for one week.

'It was not until 1964 that the name of the society was changed and this came about after an article in the local press went on to say "Crawley now has an operatic society to be proud of." Members gave some thought to this and it was decided to change the name to Crawley Operatic Society. The society continued to grow from strength to strength with outstanding successes such as *Oklahoma* in 1968. *La Belle Helène*, performed in 1973, was the last show at Sarah Robinson School.

'We had performed there for 15 years and from 1974 to 1976 five further shows were performed at Thomas Bennett School, Tilgate, St Paul's Hall, Northgate, and Hazelwick School, Three Bridges. We

Picture credit: Crawley Operatic Society

eventually settled on a new home at Thomas Bennett School for 10 years from 1977–87, and within this time took shows on tour to our twin town, Dorsten.

'We then came to our proudest moment, our first show at Crawley's new theatre, The Hawth. The first meeting to discuss the possibility of a new arts centre took place around 1966–67, so it took some 20 years to come to the first night, 10 May 1988.'

In 2007, some founder members of the society were still very much involved, some even performing on stage.

Picture credit: Crawley Operatic Society

ASHLEY SCHOOL OF DANCE

These youngsters from the Ashley School of Dance were preparing to take their bronze, silver and gold medals in 1952.

Picture credit: Marion Godsmark

The pictures belong to Marion Godsmark and she is third from left in the second picture. She thinks the girl second from the left is Georgina Gates, while the girl on the right was Miss Walley.

Ettie Rice's daughters Pauline and Jennifer were pupils at the Ashley School of Dance, as was Janet Budgen, who now lives in Crowborough. Mrs Rice named the woman on the back row of the second picture, second from the left, as Miss Ashley.

Mrs Rice, of Horley, said, 'The kids had such fun. They did a summer show in the Three Bridges Montefiore Hall and a panto at Christmas. I meet Janet every Christmas when we go to the old Three Bridges residents' party at the hall.

'We see dozens of old photographs of Three Bridges and Crawley. It is a trip down memory lane. Not the same when the new town came.'

T.S *COSSACK*

T.S. *Cossack* celebrated its 50th year afloat in 2007. This picture shows a gaggle of cadets at Crawley railway station in 1957 en route to their first summer camp in Littlehampton.

Valma Martin was able to provide a few names and offers apologies to those of whom she can only remember a surname. She said, 'After 50 years it's difficult to remember all the names. Sadly, one or two are no longer with us.'

The names she could remember were: CPO Harry Hatt, John Coad, Brian Redmond, Foster, Bob Miles, Stan Prior, Pete Simmonds, Willoughby, Buckingham, John Cook, Paul Martin, John Truscott, Drake, Hawkins, Mick Starr and Les Parker.

Picture credit: Valma Martin

REX WILLIAMS

This picture of a group of eager young scouts belongs to Rex Williams, of Turners Hill. Mr Williams is the author of *You Must Remember This*, which tells the story of Crawley during wartime through the eyes of the author as a young boy.

In the snapshot, a young Mr Williams can be seen with his fellow Crawley scouts on

Picture credit: Rex Williams

23 June 1946 being visited by General Sir Miles Dempsey. He said, 'The General presented the scouts with the pennant or flag which was flying from the bonnet of his staff car when it crossed the Rhine to take the war into Germany.

'My brother made a stand for the small flag. Its base was of polished Sussex oak and the mast had been one of my sister's wooden knitting needles.'

MARILYN CLARK

This happy bunch were certainly getting into the spirit of things when they celebrated Christmas. The picture belongs to former Crawley girl Marilyn Clark, who now lives in Hull. She said, 'This was a Christmas party at the Apple Tree in about 1956. Most of the children are from West Green. I am the one kneeling on

the left. Two away from me is Marilyn Prentice, next to her in the check dress is Angela Ansell, then Barbara Willis. Her sister is third from the right in the front row.

'Standing in the back row with her hands on her hips is Sandra Prentice. Next to the drummer, with his hat over his eyes is Greg Ansell and next to him is my brother Dave Bentley.'

Picture credit: Marilyn Clark

MARCHING BANDS

Marching bands were in their element in Crawley in the 1970s and 80s. The town held regular band competitions at the old leisure centre and bands from around town put on a great show for the spectators. Hazelwick Allstars, T.S. *Glorious* and T.S. *Tudor Rose* were just a couple of the bands who took part.

Mick Knibbs was one of the Hazelwick Allstars. He said, 'Most of the people in the pictures were from the Nautical Training Corps's T.S. *Courageous, Superb, Glorious* and *Tudor Rose*, and most of them performed in the Crawley band contest 25 years before the photograph below was taken. Back row: Roy Vanhinsbergh, Keith Wright, Ian Baker, Brian Mitchell, Diane Dawson, Terry Vanhinsbergh, Linda

Fredericks, Chris Ball, Gill Dawson, Barry Gallihawk, Claire Dawson, Mick Knibbs, Phil Austin, Phil Gill, Kev Gasson, Alan Kearsey, Bob Moore. Front row: Tom Fredericks, Colin Ellis, Graham Hurcomb, Pam Basson, Bob Ellis, Georgina Kearsey, Charlie Malthouse, Peter Kearsey.

'Most are still friends and in contact with each other even though we are spread around the country now.'

Mick owns this picture of the Crawley Carnival of around 1972 showing some of the band members when they were younger. He said, 'This band was, in its time, one of the best in the country. We won many, many band contests all over England and I was a champion drum major. I joined the NTC in 1965 at the age of 10 when I moved to Crawley from Lancing with my family, and helped even while serving in HM Forces on leave with drill, marching and deportment.

'I was invited to judge the dress and turnout at the Crawley band contest in about 1978 while serving as a L/Cpl Drummer with the Corps of Drums of the 2nd Battalion the Queens Regiment, a duty which I was honoured to carry out.

'We had band contests nearly every weekend, so our Friday evening was spent getting together and cleaning our uniforms, boots, white equipment, brasses and instruments to the highest standards.

'Lots of the members coupled up and some have been married for 30 years now. The shame of it all is that not many units of the NTC are still going in this area. T.S. *Courageous* [Ifield] and *Tudor Rose* [Langley Green] have gone, I believe, due to lack of instructors and kids. They don't seem to have the same interests as we did, and the instructors were some of our parents, most ex-military due to conscription.

'One such instructor was Roy Trebble from Langley Green. He was in the Royal Navy and what he didn't know about looking after his uniform, ironing, washing, sewing, wasn't worth knowing. That helped me a lot when joining up at the age of 15 in boy's service.'

Gina Ball and her brothers were also members of the Hazelwick Allstars. Gina, whose name at the time was Kearsey, said, 'The man in the dark jacket was called Roy Vanhinsbergh, fifth man from the left is now my husband Chris Ball, seventh from right is Mick Knibbs, next Phil Gill, another brother of mine Richard Kearsey and brother Alan Kearsey.

'Along the front from the left is Tom Fredricks, Colin Ellis, Pam Bassen, behind the man with the biggest drum is Linda Fredricks, then there's me with my special bow tie, Charlie Malthouse and yet another brother Peter Kearsey.'

If anyone knows about the Hazelwick Allstars it is Terry Vanhinsbergh, whose father formed the band. Terry wrote, 'The Hazelwick Allstars were formed from past competitors to commemorate the 25th anniversary of the Crawley Youth Marching Band Championships. The early competitions were held on the playground at Hazelwick School, hence the band's name. It comprised former members of many

local youth organisations including the Nautical Training Corps, Sea Cadet Corps, Air Training Corps, Boys' Brigade, The Overlanders, Crawley Corps of Drums, Crawley Vanguard and Masquerade.

'My dad, Roy, brought the members together to play in "the old style" with drums, bugles and bell lyres. Having guested at the Crawley Youth Marching Band Championships in 1986 he wanted us to stay together to perform at carnivals and fêtes, but it didn't happen as he died a year later.'

CRAWLEY BOYS' CLUB

Imagine how today's kids would react if David Beckham or Robbie Williams made a point of dropping in on their play centre from time to time. Crooner Frankie Vaughan was at the height of his popularity in the 1950s and 60s when the lads at Crawley Boys' Club were treated to several visits from the man himself.

Frankie was a member of the National Association of Boys' Clubs in the UK, and during his career he was a major contributor to the clubs, dedicating his monetary compensation from one song each year.

In October 1958 he took to the stage at Hazelwick School at a youth dance organised to raise cash for the Boys' Club – then based in Ifield Avenue – and it was reported that his presence caused a near riot.

The *Crawley Observer* dated 31 October reported on 'screaming girls, disparaging boys and the local police trying to keep them all under control'.

When Frankie signed autographs he borrowed a pen from 27-year-old Joan Felton, of The Dingle, West

Green, who ran his fan club. Joan was rewarded with a kiss and declared: 'I'll never use this pen again!'

The *Observer* reported: 'The first to get Frankie's autograph was 16-year-old Yolette Roberts, a Co-op girl of Donn Close, Pound Hill. What did she think of the "big man"? Same as everyone else – "S-m-a-s-h-i-n".'

In 1962 the Boys' Club moved to London Road at a cost of £25,000, and was opened by the Duke of Richmond. In November of that year Frankie returned, being welcomed by club leader Bill Ward. He had stopped off at Cloakes' record shop, in the Broadway, before going on to the club and staying through the afternoon and into the evening.

The *Observer* reported that he lifted weights in the club gym and joined a group of boys in the quiet room for a game of draughts.

A series of photographs from Crawley Boys' Club over the past five decades. The pictures include club leader Bill Ward, the opening of the club's coffee lounge which was launched in 1962 with an appeal for

more mums to go along and help, a sponsored paddle on Tilgate Lake which raised £150 for the club and amateur boxer Patrick Nelson who coached some of the boys. Today the club – now called Crawley Youth Centre – is situated on Longmere Road, West Green.

Crawley Boys' Club.

THE CONSORTS DANCE ORCHESTRA

Peter Pulling and his band provided backing music for Frankie Vaughan at Hazelwick School when he raised funds for the Boys' Club in 1958.

Mr Pulling, of Three Bridges, said: 'This photograph of my band, The Consorts Dance Orchestra, was taken on the night when we backed Frankie for about five or six numbers, including his chart hit *Green Door*. I formed The Consorts in 1954 and managed the band until 1987. I am now 80 years young and I have happy memories of the musicians and vocalists who played with me at functions all over Sussex, Surrey and London.

'We were a very popular and successful semi-pro band. We played the Frankie Vaughan show for free.'

Picture credit: Peter Pulling

GUIDES

This fascinating collection of pictures was picked up at an antiques fair by Peter Allen.

According to the information that came with the album, the photographs show the 2nd Crawley company, captained by Miss Marjorie Stanford (dated 13 December 1938) and the 1st Crawley pack at which Miss Stanford was Brown Owl (dated 26 February 1948).

A newspaper cutting paid tribute to Miss Stanford when she retired from the Guides. It read: 'One of the pioneers of the Girl Guide movement in Crawley, Miss M. Stanford, relinquished the captaincy of the 2nd Crawley Company. She had spent 33 years altogether in the Guides, which she and Mrs Martley, wife of the then vicar of St Peter's, started in 1910. Miss Stanford retired from the Guides for a period owing to ill health, returning as Ranger Captain.

'High tribute was paid to Miss Stanford's work when the Guides held an open evening at Goffs Hall. Jane Turner, on behalf of the Guides, said they were all very sad to say goodbye to Miss Stanford. They thanked her for all she had done for the company and the encouragement she had given. Elizabeth Davies welcomed Miss Douglas, a member of the staff at Crawley Development Corporation, who is taking over the captaincy.'

Picture credit: Peter Allen

Picture credit: Peter Allen

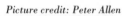

Picture credit: Peter Allen

On her retirement Miss Stanford was presented with a card which read: 'To Miss Stanford, In appreciation of your long and devoted service to the Guide movement. All our best wishes for the future.' The Guides had signed the card, some of the names being: Barbara Barratt, Julia Harvey, Jane Turner, Ann Allen, Eileen Foster, Beryl Parsons, Mary Law, Barbara Hewsey, Stella Henry, Elizabeth Davies, Valerie Strevett, Daphne Allen, Sheila Knight, Pat Dean and Janet Moors.

Among the photographs in Mr Allen's album was a Proficiency Badge Certificate which declared that the 2nd Crawley Guide Company had passed the required tests for the Plays (second word indecipherable) badge.

It was signed by R.M. Trower of the Crawley Drama Group and noted: 'This company does first-class work'.

The certificate carried two dates, 1 April 1952 and 5 July 1952 (marked DOB, perhaps Date of Badge?).

THE 852 BUS

David Ralph, of Bewbush, has fond memories of the 852 bus which used to drop its passengers at Ifield station. He said: 'The 852 bus isn't just a distant memory of old Crawley as my brother, Tim, and I own one of these lovely old London Transport buses. It is one of 84 such buses built for London Transport in

1953. They were used in villages and towns on lightly used routes or where larger buses would have difficulty through narrow roads.

'The route 852 ran from Crawley High Street out to Ifield, Ifield Wood, Lambs Green, Faygate, Horsham and on to Ewhurst in Surrey. Tim and I have rebuilt the bus from poor condition and now use it regularly for shows and to take friends or family on days out.'

BRITISH AND WORLD MARBLES CHAMPIONSHIPS

Say what you like about Crawley, it is not a town that can be accused of losing its marbles. Every Good Friday, the Greyhound Pub in Tinsley Green plays host to the British and World Marbles

Championships. The event is hugely popular and sees teams from across the globe descend on Crawley armed with their shooters and mibs.

These pictures from the *Crawley Observer* archives show players from 1984 and 1985 knuckling down at the Greyhound.

The older pictures show George 'Pop' Maynard, arguably Crawley's most famous player. Sam McCarthy-Fox, writing on The Marble Museum website at *www.marblemuseum.org* said of Pop: 'A figure synonymous with Tinsley Green and the marbles championships was George "Pop" Maynard, captain of the Copthorne Spitfires. Pop was born in Smallfields just over the Surrey border but it was

not long after that his family moved to Copthorne, where he remained for the rest of his long life.

'He first gained national recognition in 1948 when the Copthorne Spitfires won the team event and Pop appeared on TV. He was also a well-known folk-singer and was recorded by the BBC. Some of his songs can be heard on a Topic record.

'Pop was 82 years old when he first flew and it was with George

Burbridge and the Tinsley Tigers to Le Touquet, France. They were guests of the Mayor and Corporation of the town and gave exhibitions of marbles in the town and on the beach. A year later in 1955 he opened a marbles ring at Jordans, in the London Road; he did it by dropping a marble into the ring from a three-seater Bell helicopter.

'In his latter years Pop suffered with arthritis in his hand, but he could still knock the last marble from the ring right up to the end. He died in 1962 at the age of 90.'

4TH WORTH CUBS IN 1952

Scouting is supposed to be fun and this bunch of cheeky chappies certainly seem to be having a good time. The picture was sent in by Pete Allen and the boys were members of the 4th Worth Cubs in 1952. The group is based in Three Bridges but its website *www.4thworthscouts.org.uk* explains the name. It reads, 'The idea of Scouting quickly gained interest all over the country and in 1908 a Dr Willett, together with others, formed scout troops for the boys living in the parish of Worth, which at the time stretched from beyond Turners Hill in the east up to a small stream, now piped in, that runs just to the east of where Crawley College stands today – the point where Three Bridges Road joins Haslett Avenue.

'The parish covered an area that included Turners Hill, Crawley Down, Paddockhurst/Worth Abbey and part of Copthorne.

Picture credit: Peter Allen

'Originally the troops formed had the name "Worth" in their title, so Crawley Down was 1st Worth, Turners Hill 2nd Worth, Copthorne 3rd Worth and the troop for the boys living near Worth Church and in Three Bridges was named 4th Worth. Collectively the troops were known to the Boy Scouts Association as the Worth District Scout Association.'

The 4th Worth is the only troop to have kept its name. A lack of leaders at the outbreak of World War One led to the disbanding of the other three, but they later re-formed using the name of their village.

CRAWLEY MILITARY BAND IN 1954

Picture credit: Brian Mitchell

room with him, so it brings back some very pleasant memories.'

THE SECOND CRAWLEY YOUTH BAND

This photograph shows the assembly of bands at the second Crawley Youth Band held at Hazelwick School in 1963.

Picture credit: Brian Mitchell

Brian Mitchell said: 'As you will see the uniforms of the scouts still included short trousers and the band in bearskins were The Overlanders who came from Crawley. I was involved on the organising committee as a member of T.S. *Courageous*, Nautical Training Corps based at the Old Mill in Ifield and the committee were under the chairmanship of Major Jack East, ACF.'

SQUIRE'S DRUM AND BUGLE CORPS

There is nothing like music to bring people together, and back in the 1980s one man did a huge amount to get Crawley youngsters involved. Squire's Drum and Bugle Corps owe a lot to Robert Gillett and his family for the effort they put into running the group from 1987.

Band member Jodie Fuller said, 'Robert Gillett and his family were heavily involved in running the corps on a day-to-day basis and put in a lot of hard work, personal time and effort to keep this going and did so up until recent years. It is with great thanks to Rob and his family that the Squire's Drum and Bugle Corps have given an amazing opportunity and skills in music and dance for many young people across Crawley and Sussex.'

The Corps was started for the youth of Crawley of all ages and all abilities in 1987.

Jodie said, 'It was a charity organisation and members, parents and many committed fundraisers helped this marching band grow from strength to strength throughout the years. There was a cadet corps and a senior corps with ages ranging from five years to 22 years plus.

'Parents of the members helped on a weekly basis with

Picture credit: Squire's Drum and Bugle Corps

equipment, instruments, uniforms and welfare of members, creating a family-like and caring environment for all.

'Music, dance, showmanship and competitive spirit were taught by music professionals and experience passed down through the generations of members and staff alike, to make this local marching band a great organisation to be a part of.

'The Squires travelled all over the country and into Europe in competition and did extremely well in the world of DCUK [Drum Corps United Kingdom] every year.'

JUNIOR IMPERIAL LEAGUE

When the new town was built, a range of social clubs were formed for the new residents and rightly so – a new home in a new town with no friends can be painfully lonely. But before World War Two, these old towners had a club of their own based in the Guides' hut on Horsham Road.

Picture credit: Frederick Bingham

This picture of the Junior Imperial League – known as the Imps – belongs to Frederick Bingham and he thinks it was snapped around 1938. Mr Bingham said 'It was run by the Conservatives and we had to listen to lectures. We also used to go all around the countryside and take our tea with us. We were the only club in Crawley and we had dances every week.'

Mr Bingham remembers that Miss Hopkins was the club president and named Helen Brackpool, Jack Skinner, Ruth Delamer, Roy Cheesmur, Miss Martin and Miss Begbie. Also in the picture is Lady Dorothy Longley.

THE STARLIGHT BALLROOM

It was labelled an eyesore and now there is nothing left of it apart from its footprint, but, for those who grew up in Crawley in the 1960s and 70s, Sussex House was the place to be seen.

Sue Vincent, of Tilgate, has very fond memories of the building – then known rather romantically as the Starlight Ballroom – and remembers the exhausting feat that was a dance marathon which was held there in May of 1969 or 1970.

Her sister Elaine danced for almost a day and finished very early on the Sunday morning while Vic Jones – a lad with an awful lot of staying power – won the marathon having danced for some 48 hours from Friday to Sunday. Sue said, 'You had to keep moving your arms and legs and you got a 10-minute

break every hour. Colin Berry DJ'd on the Saturday during the marathon. He kept saying "arms, Sue, arms!" because I was tired and forgot to move them.'

For taking part, Sue received a tiny gold Coca-Cola bottle – which she keeps on a bracelet – and a three-month pass to the Starlight.

The Starlight played host to an impressive line-up of big names over the years.

Some of the superstars to grace the stage included: The Who, 24 March 1966; The Iveys, 26 March 1967 and 31 March 1967; Pink Floyd, 23 April 1967; The Iveys, 14 May 1967 and 20 August 1967; Strange Band, 7 September; The Move, 1 October 1967; Family Bandstand, 7 September 1967; Jimi Hendrix, 15 October 1967; Small Faces, 24 October 1967; The Who, 11 February 1968; Mott The Hoople, 3 and 12 January 1971; Uriah Heep, 2 February 1971; Genesis, 11 February 1971; Status Quo, 16 February 1971 (Chuck Berry is listed for the same date); Hawkwind, 25 May 1971; Van der Graaf Generator, 20 July 1971; Status Quo, 28 September 1971; Uriah Heep, 19 October 1971.

Sue said: 'When the Small Faces came, I can remember standing on a chair and leaning on some guy and screaming and shouting. I went by myself at 16. I remember the Easy Beats, who were Australian, asking a couple of girls to go up and help to play the tambourine.'

There was always something happening in the Ballroom and Sue remembers many a disco and more than one bout of wrestling being held there. She said, 'I would have been still at school when I saw Mick McManus. I used to go with my mum – who was very enthusiastic! I remember seeing Shirley Crabtree before he became Big Daddy. It was either babysit for my brother or go wrestling.'

While the wrestling was held downstairs, there was a disco upstairs. Sue said, 'You could see right down onto the ring and sometimes they would tell us to turn the music down. They boarded the windows up eventually.'

On Wednesday afternoons there were discos at the Starlight. Many of the shops in Crawley used to close on Wednesday afternoons, so the staff would head for the disco.

There were also discos in the evening and Sue and her Woolworths colleagues – Irene Sloane, Pauline Rainbow and Lyn Stocker – would work until 7pm, get changed at work and go to the disco at 7.30pm. 'Wages were £7 and tickets were the equivalent of 75p so I would wait to see what I could afford.'

Some big-name DJs of the time often joined in the fun and Sue remembers seeing Pete Drummond and BBC Radio 1 legend Anne Nightingale. 'I remember one time when all the teens were watching The Johnny Howard Band and the older people were dancing waltzes around them.'

Picture credit: Sue Vincent

The disco was named the Bear Pit in the 1970s and, after Sue had her son, she went to work there serving food. The Bear Pit closed in October 1975.

After moving to Crawley in 1959, Sue went to Sarah Robinson School in Ifield and remembers when future boxing legend Alan Minter played the part of a prince in the school play of 1962–63.

Along with her sister Elaine, she was a go-go dancer: 'We used to wear a top with fringing and white pleated trousers. We used to go in the bowling alley when there was a fashion show and model Pippa Dee clothes. I only ever bowled once and even then I had the bumpers up. The Starlight Ballroom was open from Friday to Sunday. The ballroom was lovely when it opened.'

Before the Starlight became the place to go for good music in days gone by, there was the Mojo R'n'B Club, which is remembered by Bob Rashbrook, of Southgate. He said, 'This was situated where the Jehovah's Witness Kingdom Hall is in Northgate, opposite Northgate Parade. The likes of the late Long John Baldry and the Graham Bond Organisation played there. The legendary Jack Bruce and Ginger Baker – later of Cream – played with Graham Bond in them days.

'On a Friday evening, Northgate was the centre point in Crawley when the Mojo was open and there were people everywhere, and not a police officer in sight, except one night when Bond was playing and a police officer had the thankless task of trying to get the band to turn down the volume!

'Apart from the Mojo Club in the 60s, the Civic Hall was another great venue for bands. They held clubs there on Fridays and Sundays. I believe the Sunday club was more commonly called the U2 Club. I can remember The Who, The Pretty Things, Them (lead singer Van Morrison), The Spencer Davis Group (lead singer Stevie Winwood), The Merseybeats and many more playing there.

'Not only did we have the Civic Hall, but most weekends there was something going on at other venues such as old Crawley Boys' Club, where the like of local bands The Daltons and The Jaguars played.

'Ifield School was another popular venue that saw the likes of Lulu, Johnny Kidd and the Pirates (Johnny died in a car accident in October 1966), The Honeycombs (a unique band as they had a girl drummer!) and Horsham band The Beat Merchants.

'In later years the Starlight Ballroom was the key venue and may bands performed there, The Small Faces, The Hollies and The Sensational Alex Harvey Band, to name a few.

'You had your odd hiccup but nothing serious enough for the riot squad to be called and these venues were all alcohol free.'

GOSSOPS GREEN CARNIVAL

Remember the days when the word 'carnival' meant floats and fancy dress and the community coming together to produce an event that was fun for all?

These pictures were taken in May 1969 and show some of the people who took part in the Gossops Green Carnival. According to a newspaper cutting of the time, the smiles may have been sunny but the weather was not: 'Saturday's Gossops Green Carnival, like all new town activities at the weekend, was affected by the bad weather. But with the use of Gossops Green Community Centre and breaks in the rain everything went off quite smoothly.'

Here we have the St Alban's Church Young Wives, who were showing off their 1920s fashions,

complete with bangles, baubles and beads, and a group of children peering into the Community Centre window to see what is going on.

Next is David Frampton dressed as Jack from *Jack and the Beanstalk*. David was representing the Gossops Green Gardening Club and his colourful float came complete with a goose and its golden egg. The lads of Kidborough United FC were full of good cheer despite the fact they were missing a televised international football match.

PEOPLE

MRS H.C. CARMAN MBE JP

As well as being chairman of Crawley Urban District Council, Hepzibah Carman was a magistrate and penned a book in 1968 called *As The Old Ones Knew It*, a personal view of life in Crawley pre-new town.

The following is an extract from the book:

'The George was a great centre at the time. The older people talked of ostlers and fine horses bringing coaches from London via Reigate to Brighton regularly, but in my young days there were only the luxury trips by "Vanderbilt" which ran to Brighton in the summer months.

'We could hear the Post Horn proclaiming as it came by the Half Moon at Hoggs Hill on its way from Brighton, and as we were leaving school, if we were quick, we might get down to the George in time to see the changing of the horses and the "foine folk" coming out after their brief stay for refreshment and comfort. The Shades was in the main the public bar, for lesser folks.

'Until 1914 we had celebrated Bonfire Night, 5 November, with a torchlight procession and then a bonfire in the square, opposite the George Hotel. When Macadam was used, the bonfire had to be transferred to a field behind the White Hart to avoid the risk of hefty conflagration arising from the tarred surface.

'Our first motor accident was on the narrow Ifield Road at the spot where Warren Drive cuts across old Ifield Road.

'In 1928 the two parishes of Crawley and Ifield were joined and we had 15 councillors. At one election there were 25 councillors and the voting paper had that number of names on it (once I came 25th).

'On the night of the Fire of London (29–30 December 1940) we stood on our front porches gazing to the north-east watching the blaze in the sky and knowing something

Picture credit: Rae Carman

mighty awful was happening. Next morning a brother confirmed the rumours (he had been standing on London Bridge on a return journey to Crawley when it happened).'

ALICIA HOWARD

A decades-old bottle of champagne which was won by a four-year-old girl in a *Crawley Observer* balloon competition in the 1950s was still waiting to be drunk by its owner in 2006. When Alicia Howard won the bubbly after her balloon flew the furthest in a competition organised by the paper at Crawley parish church fête in August 1956, her mother, unsurprisingly, said they would keep it until she was old enough to drink it.

The following year, Alicia and her sister, Rachel, were pictured by an *Observer* photographer at the fête advertising that year's competition and, although she did not win, she kept the cutting, photograph and the bottle of champagne. It stayed with her family throughout the years amid numerous moves and ended up at Alicia's home in Bosham, near Chichester, where she lived with her husband and three children.

There never seemed to be an important enough occasion on which to open the bottle and when Alicia rediscovered the photograph and yellowing cutting from 2 August 1957, in a box of family documents, she said, 'My family moved to Crawley when I was a toddler, first renting a house, Old Martyrs, and then moving to a shop at 4 Robinson Road – Howards – which my parents, John and Mary Howard, ran as a newspaper, tobacconists and general shop until early 1959. It was owned by a Mrs Hoggard and one room was sub-let to a bookmaker.

'I remember the boys' school opposite our shop, with its lily ponds which I fell into, the glove factory next door to us, the congregational church further along Robinson Road where we went to Sunday school and some old houses with big gardens, where we played, at the end of the road.

'As the railway line ran along the back of our garden, I could look out of my bedroom window and see the smoke of steam trains above the hedge.

'My sister, who is 15 months older than me, and I went to school at St John's Lodge, a small private school, which was owned by Miss Florence Ridge with a teacher, Mrs Towle. We also went to Brownies, run by Pat Pilbeam. There was a friendly butcher nearby, Compton I think his name was, and other tradespeople my parents knew who added up to a community clustered around the old town centre.

'We were all quite sorry to leave Crawley, but, for various reasons, my parents intended to emigrate. However, that fell through and in June 1959 we moved to Portsmouth where my parents ran several businesses over the next 25 years. My sister went to work in Hong Kong and I became a journalist.

'When I visited Crawley, I was rather sad to realise the Asda store had been built on the site of my old home and I could recognise very few places, apart from St John's Church, but at least I have my bottle of champagne to remember a happy childhood.

'Perhaps I'm old enough to open the bottle now; although I'm not confident it will be worth drinking after all these years!'

POLICE OFFICER

The long arm of the law was comfortably visible on the streets of Crawley during the 1950s and this officer seems to be doing a good job of keeping what traffic there was flowing.

This picture belongs to Tony Syrett, who was confident the officer was still living in Pound Hill in 2007.

Picture credit: Tony Syrett

JOHN PESKETT

Take a close look at this picture. It was taken in a perfectly normal garden in Malthouse Road, Southgate, but the structure on the left of the picture is not a shed.

The pictures belong to Deborah Powers, whose aunt, Heather Peskett, still lived in the house in 2007. She said 'She still lives in the original house with a coal fire, no central heating and only a bit of double glazing. She was 81 in 2007.'

Picture credit: Deborah Powers

As for the railway carriage – it was placed there because Deborah's grandfather used to work for the railways. Deborah said, 'It was brought up on a flat-bed truck. There used to be allotments at the end of the gardens – Beeches Crescent wasn't there yet. People from the Bluebell Railway came by years ago and took bits from it that they needed for their railway. It's still there to this day. She keeps all sorts in it.'

Deborah was born in Canada but moved back and forth to Crawley due to her father's job, before settling here for good in 1974. Her family's connection with the town runs deep and even a shopping trip to Asda brings back memories. Her aunt Stella lived in the end house in Robinson Road – the spot now occupied by the big tree in the supermarket grounds.

Picture credit: Deborah Powers

Deborah's grandfather, John Peskett, was a highly respected man. Seen here with his wife Jessie, a keen gardener, at his side on their Golden Wedding anniversary, he carried out his duties as a clerk for British Railways, was a member of the parish council from 1945–55, secretary of the Crawley Labour Party for 13 years, chairman and captain of Popes Mead Bowling Club and an extremely popular governor at Gossops Green Infants' School in the 1960s. In 1947 he hosted a Welcome Home dinner and social at the Sun Hotel for men and women returning home from service during World War Two. John died in 1976.

THE CHANTLERS

Colin Edgar is a Crawley man through and through and has traced his family line – the Chantlers – back to the 18th century. His research has turned up some fascinating characters, and anyone who has enjoyed a pint in the Brewery Shades has shared a little bit of Chantler history.

The earliest record of the Chantlers comes with Ephraim (1797–1862), who is buried at Charlwood church. His youngest son, George, had the biggest impact on Crawley. A travelling shoemaker by trade, George, along with his wife Amelia and son Leonard, moved back to Crawley in the 1850s and took up residence at 21 Crawley Street, to the right of the Sun Inn.

Mr Edgar wrote, 'In 1871 George purchased the properties 83–87 the High Street [now the Shades and the little adjoining shop]. These were a brewery, small flat and house with small shop and

Picture credit: Colin Edgar

cottage. The land with it went back to just before the old site of the bandstand in Queens Square.

'Nos 87 and 85 were purchased freehold but 83, the brewery, was sold as leasehold.

'The charge was £22 per acre and he had to have a £500 insurance policy and ensure the outside was painted annually. Although he had an income from his shoemaking business, it is strongly believed he borrowed money initially from his sister-in-law Ruth Coates née Morley. She owned property in the High

Street consisting of a toymaking and confectionery shop. She later moved to 24 Horsham Road, now the Casbah, and traded from there until her death in 1900.

'By 1874 George was really showing what an entrepreneur he was as Kelly's *History of Sussex* [Crawley] records him as a bootmaker, brewer, coal merchant and retailer of malt and hops.

'Leonard assisted him in these tasks until he married in 1883 after which he then "never did a day's work again". George had a house built, Lion Villa, at Tushmore – now the site of a roundabout – and gave it to Leonard and his wife, Elsie, to live in. He also purchased three cottages to the north, now the site of flat-topped houses, which he let out.'

In 1887 – the year Scotland beat England 3–2 in the Home Championships – the people of Crawley downed their last pint of 'Chantlers'. George sold the brewery to G. Dean, landlord of the Swan at West Green.

Mr Edgar wrote, 'George turned his hand to dealing in furniture, some of which he made himself. After eight years of banging his thumb with a hammer he opened the shop as a drapers in 1905. Two years prior to this, Leonard and family moved to Langley Lane, Ifield, to a farm called Vine Cottage and later Little Ducksford, but due to lack of space his eldest child Alice (Biddy) went to live with George and Amelia. She helped with the drapery business. In 1909, aged 75, Amelia died and was buried in Ifield churchyard. Leonard's second daughter Lilian then moved to 87 High Street to assist Alice and George. When George died on 4 February 1911 – at a sprightly 81 – Lion Villa and the Tushmore cottages were sold and the proceeds were used to pay off all moneys owing on the High Street and Langley Lane properties. The High Street property was left in its entirety to Alice.

'Alice continued, along with Lilian, to run a drapery business in the High Street changing to fruit and veg dealers in 1928. A small part of the building (front left) was sold to a Mr Thompsett of West Green for him to run a shoe shop around 1938.

'In 1947 the buildings and land were subject to a compulsory purchase order by the New Towns Commission so they could develop the area that is now Queens Square. The whole property was bought for just over £2,000 and the shop was then rented back to the sisters. The rents charged and the prices paid for High Street properties caused a few old Crawley traders to shut up shop. Alice and Lilian were very poor business people and gave out a lot of credit so their wealth soon declined. In the mid-1950s they sold out the fruit and veg shop to a Mr Young but continued to live upstairs until their deaths, Lilian in 1957 and Alice in 1974. On her demise Alice left just £100. Both were spinsters.'

RADISH THE HORSE

Meet a very important member of the Chantler clan – Radish the horse (1872–1887).

You must have heard of Radish – he is the horse who held the prestigious Flying Firkin trophy – for getting beer from Crawley to the Star at Rusper still in a drinkable condition – for five years, between 1874–78. He and George Chantler were quite a team.

In his notes, Mr Edgar wrote, 'Radish was born in the manor of Ifield in a barn that stood in a field on the left-hand side of the old Ifield road where the sports and social club now is [Crawley Rugby Club], just before Ifield brook passes under the road. Of excellent stock, one of his cousins was reputedly runner-up in the 1874 Derby!

'Selected for his stamina as well as his obvious good looks, Radish began his working life in early 1873 and was soon a very popular figure on the daily beer runs with George. He was always ready with a

Picture credit: Colin Edgar

friendly whinny and not the slightest bit camera shy, as the two examples show. Extremely well fed, his dung was highly sought-after as a garden fertilizer. If you check back through Crawley Horticultural Society's records, you will find that the rose section made regular forays to his stable with their buckets!

Picture credit: Colin Edgar

'A loyal servant to the family, Radish was retired in 1885 and spent the rest of his days quietly in the orchard at the rear of the brewery.'

1960s BIKERS

These intimidating-looking lads were snapped at County Oak by an *Observer* photographer in the early 1960s.

The other two pictures were dug up by Marilyn Clark, who now lives in Hull. She said, 'The photographs were taken at the Blue Pencil Café on County Oak in about 1963. I think the Ibis Hotel now stands on the site. All the local bikers used to meet there. I think the *Observer's* article was about the owner welcoming the bikers and giving them a room to use which they then had the job of decorating.'

'The guy with the paint brush was Pete Casey and third from the right is my brother Dave Bentley.'

Picture credit: Marilyn Clark

This photograph was taken in 1969 at West Green Youth Club, which was held at the time in St Peter's hall in Alpha Road, later moving to West Green Community Centre.

In the photograph below are, from left: Dave Taylor, Ann (who later became his wife), Rod Thatcher, Ed Wakefield, Ron Brackpool (owner of the bike), Les Brown (youth club leader), Barry Edwards and Mick Pragnell.

With their leather jackets and motorbike, the lads looked every inch the tough rockers – but, according to their families and friends, they were genuine nice guys. Speaking about Dave Taylor, Rowena Palmer, of Pound Hill, said 'He looks so hard in the picture but he is such a lovely bloke. He would have been about 18 – he was a real rocker!'

Rowena said that Dave lives in Lincolnshire now and runs a one-man delivery business. Dave and Ann have two grown-up children and the rocker from the 1960s is now a proud granddad.

Eddie Wakefield was one of the young bikers in 1963. He said 'I was known by most people those days by my nickname, Jonah. The bike at the youth club was a 250cc Royal Enfield Continental GT.

'The group line-up photograph I remember well, although I am not in it. I was actually pulling into the Blue Pencil on my motorcycle as it was taken – late again, which was not unusual!'

Peter Thomas Gaby, of Ontario, Canada, said, 'I grew up in Crawley, in Five Acres Road, Hazelwick school etc. The Blue Pencil and Mario's Cafe in the town centre were hang-outs for us motorcycle types – "Ton Up Boys"…only I couldn't afford a motor cycle that would do the magic ton (100mph) at that time.

Picture credit: Marilyn Clark

'Another of our pals was the well-known motorcycle racer Malcolm Dearn – "Munch" on account of the large quantity of food he could consume. Malcolm was tragically killed in a motor accident in 2007.

'I still ride the good old British bikes and have a small collection of machines from that "rocker" period, but we call ourselves the "Geriatric Ton Up Boys" now – a lot of talk but not much go!

'The Blue Pencil was a well-known motorcycle stopping point for riders coming down from London en route to Brighton. If you had a quick bike one could make the Pillars/Gates at the Brighton city line in 20 minutes from Crawley, averaging 60mph. It took some doing as the A23 was only part dual carriageway in those days.'

PERCY AND MARGARET EMMERSON

Percy and Margaret Emmerson certainly had a lot to smile about as the 1950s drew to a close. The devoted couple were crowned *Crawley Courier* Happy Couple on 28 May 1957 at the Railway Hotel after winning a contest published in the paper.

The contest was run as part of the Crawley Carnival and a souvenir programme would set you back one shilling. Couples had to fill out a questionnaire and write in no more than 200 words why they were the Happy Couple. The contest offered £70 worth of prizes.

Mrs Emmerson, who was 95 in 2007, had clear memories of the competition. 'Gert and Daisy Walters judged it and there were special judges. We were overwhelmed. We had to stand up and tell them why

Picture credit: Margaret Emmerson

Picture credit: Margaret Emmerson

Picture credit: Margaret Emmerson

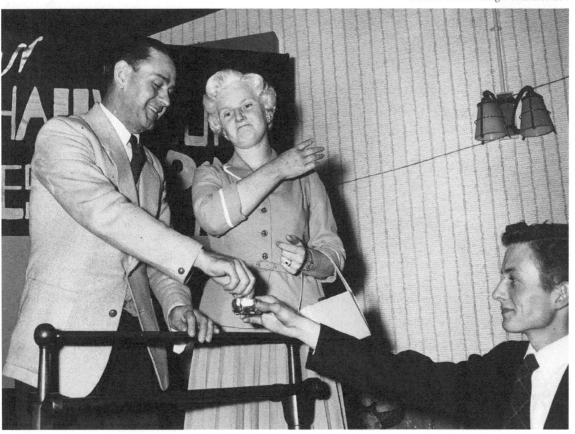

Picture credit: Margaret Emmerson

we were happy. We were interviewed separately. It was all done properly. The councillors were there in their wigs. The names went into the pot and ours came out first.'

Mr and Mrs Emmerson's prize was a weekend in Paris – accompanied by *Courier* reporter Peter Avis, who acted as their guide.

According to the programme, the judges for the day were Elsie and Doris Waters – known as Gert and Daisy – and Avril Angers. The clerk of the court was John Standen and the usher was Michael Older.

A picture appeared in the *Courier's* carnival coverage showing Mr Emmerson giving the Carnival Queen a kiss. The caption read: 'She seemed to be enjoying the idea anyway, though she did have to hold her crown on. Mr Emmerson ended this charming ceremony with lipstick smeared on his cheek, much to the amusement of Mrs Emmerson.'

Of the other contestants, Mr and Mrs W. Stewart came fourth, Mr and Mrs G. Isaac came third and Mr and Mrs T. Thew came second.

At the time, the *Courier* was based at 9 High Street and went on sale on Friday and cost threepence.

BAND AID

In 1985, Britain was gripped by Band Aid fever. People from all over Crawley pitched in to raise money. Kids from schools helped raise money for designated charities and there was a Band Aid concert held at the Goffs Park Hotel, where band Sandown performed.

THE SALVATION ARMY

'This is my story, this is my song. Praising my saviour all the day long...' This was the refrain to the hymn *Blessed Assurance*, sung at the local meetings of the Salvation Army in Crawley in the early 1950s.

This picture of the women of Crawley Salvation Army in the early 1950s belongs to Susan Trachsel-Farmer, of Switzerland. Susan left Crawley to live abroad but often popped back to England to see her family and visit Crawley, where her parents and grandparents are buried. Her mother, Dorothy Farmer née Best, served as an usher at the Embassy Cinema where she met her future husband, Leslie. Leslie was an inspector at Crawley Post Office. Dorothy died in 1997.

Susan said, 'I have fond memories of attending those weekly get-togethers with my mother at the local community hall complete with its old-fashioned – but how very trendy – woodburning stove. I believe Asda now stands on the grounds. Being pre-school age, I didn't understand what the Salvation Army was all about, but I loved the ladies' hats with the frilly red ribbon.

'In the photograph, my mother is on the left in the front row and my paternal grandmother, Rose Farmer, is in the centre of the middle row.'

The Salvation Army was founded by Methodist minister William Booth in 1865. Instead of waiting for people to come to the church he took the church to the people, travelling throughout the land preaching to thieves, prostitutes, gamblers and alcoholics.

Picture credit: Susan Trachsel-Farmer

THE NEW CITY JAZZMEN

For nearly as long as there has been a new town there has been a bandstand in Queens Square, and one of the best bands to entertain the shoppers over the decades celebrated its 50th anniversary in 2007. The New City Jazzmen is the oldest established traditional jazz band in the south of England and was formed in Crawley in 1957.

Describing the band's early days, founder member Bernard Hodgson said, 'A bunch of aspiring jazz musicians started practising in an empty bakery under the El Salvador coffee bar at No.6 Brighton Road and the

All Pictures: New City Jazzmen

band played its first public date in a dance hall above Leon's dress shop on the north-west corner of Queens Square on 25 September 1957.

'It christened the newly-erected bandstand in Queens Square in 1958 and has clocked up thousands of appearances in the town over the last 50 years.'

The amazing thing is the longevity of most of the musicians in the band. Mr Hodgson, who plays the trumpet, trombonist Ron Westcott, pianist Mike Godfrey and bassist Alan Kennington were there right at the beginning. Clarinettist Chris Jaques joined in 1963, banjo player Sluff Hazell in 1965 and drummer Barry Lewis in 1976. The remaining member is vocalist Penny Payne, who joined the band in 1995.

The band has issued five CDs and the story of the band appears in the book *New City Jazzmen: The Story*. In Bernard Hodgson's book, councillor Jim Smith, a self confessed New City Jazz fan and president of Crawley Arts Council, said this in his foreword: 'The New City Jazzmen are an institution...or is it that they should be in an institution? These chaps have been entertaining the people of Crawley and many others from far and wide for so many years. Their stage was, and still is any pub, hall, room or theatre that will accommodate them.

The band had their own little 'tour bus'.

In 1972, a Crawley Festival of Arts was held and enough money was allocated to jazz for the group to have Humphrey Lyttleton, Cuff Billet and the Chris Barber Band on three separate evenings. The most popular solo performance was that of George Chisholm (trombone) in May 1972. He travelled by train and the group had arranged for Mike Godfrey to meet him at Three Bridges station. His train was late, but there were loads

of people in the Grasshopper, so they started playing. At 8.15pm he arrived and walked down the centre of the hall to a cheer. Climbing on to the bandstand, he immediately started unpacking his trombone.

'Wouldn't you like to have a quick drink at the bar and get your breath,' Bernard Hodgson asked. 'No,' he said with a grin, 'I'm here to play so let's play.'

Musician Stan Worboys often deputised for Alan Kennington when he could not make a gig.

He said: 'After leaving the Metropole I played for many years at the Brighton Grand Hotel with Geoff Simkins. Following the IRA bombing, the police asked me if I remembered 15 September. This was the date they thought the bomb was planted. I said "Yes, very well." "Oh! Why was that?" they asked. "It was my birthday and I had to buy the band a beer," I said. But I didn't talk to any Irishmen, so I was of no help to the police.

'As a freelance bass player, I get some interesting gigs. A last-minute call from Benny Simkins [Geoff's late father] resulted in a recording session with Yank Lawson, of World's Greatest Jazzband fame. He came without his band to play with musicians from Europe. Geoff and Pete were, of course, in their dad's band – also Roy Bower and the late Mike Collier. The drummer Vic Richards and clarinettist Randy Colville have also passed on.

'This recording at Ted Taylor's studio was issued on the Flyright label. That was 1979 – vinyl in those days.

'At an outdoor gig with the New City Jazzmen some years ago the bride and groom left the tented reception in a hot air balloon to the tune *Up Up and Away in my Beautiful Balloon*. There are so many stories.'

THE OCTOBER STORM OF '87

Do you remember where you were when the October Storm of '87 did its best to blow the south of England off the map?

Given the hour, you were probably in bed, but quite a few people were unable to sleep that night. Winds of up to 100kph battered the south, uprooting trees and tossing roof tiles about like confetti.

The people of Crawley came through that tempestuous night more or less unscathed, though their property was not quite so lucky.

The *Observer* of 21 October reported how a man got his family to safety after a tree fell on their house in Coppice Walk, Three Bridges, only to narrowly avoid being hit by a second tree when he went back to check on the family dog. The wind also tore off the roof of the house. David Fixter said at the time 'It didn't surprise me. The wind was very strong.'

A family of four spent the night in the police canteen when officers evacuated them from their Caburn Heights home after the storm blew down their attic wall.

Gales Drive in Three Bridges lived up to its name when a tree was brought crashing down onto a house and £4,000 of damage was caused to a 250-year old cottage in Ifield when a large poplar smashed into the roof.

One particularly unlucky couple were left with a huge clean-up job when six trees fell in their garden and a seventh went through their roof.

Audrey and Barrie Moor, of Pound Hill, were full of praise for their neighbours, who rushed to help.

Audrey said at the time: 'They were fantastic and worked like Trojans. Our house must be the most photographed in Crawley now.'

A Three Bridges grocer had a narrow escape when a tree crashed through the roof of his van – just as he was about to move it.

Tilgate Park did not escape unharmed, either, with one area south of the main lawn destroyed and the Victorian Pinetum badly damaged.

CRAWLEY AND HORSHAM POLICE

The long arm of the law was certainly well turned-out in the 1950s, as this picture shows.

It belongs to Ian Hands and shows the men of the Crawley and Horsham police gathered for their annual ball. Mr Hands thinks the picture was taken in the early 1950s at Gatwick Manor. He said: 'The sergeant went on to become the assistant chief constable.'

Picture credit: Ian Hands

'UNCLE' TOM PARRY

This picture shows one of Crawley's 'Uncles' chatting to a young lad at Southgate Play Centre.

The Uncles are long gone from the Crawley entertainment circuit, but generations of children remember them with fondness. Bob Rashbrook, of Southgate, said, 'His name is Tom Parry. Tom lived for many years prior to his death in Railey Road, Northgate. My association with Tom was through football where he was a referee and a member of the Sussex County Football Association as a council member. This I'm clear about because I replaced him on being elected to that council.

'My first recollection of him was when he refereed a game I played in at West Green Junior School. I was a member of the all-conquering Northgate School of 1959 who played a Crawley Schools Select team. It was the first game I played in with a "proper" referee.'

ST JOHN AMBULANCE CADETS

This picture shows the members of St John Ambulance Cadets in around 1938. The cadets formed in 1935 and this group were the first class in Crawley. Lessons were held in Mr Cooper's house in Cross Keys.

Pictured from left are Bert Cooper, Mr Cooper, Dennis Williams, Pat Davies, Alf Picking and Mick Langridge.

Picture credit: Peter Allen

CRAWLEY CAKE AND BISCUIT FACTORY

These two dapper gents were snapped with their fantastic old delivery van outside the Crawley Cake and Biscuit Factory in the 1930s. The factory stood on Ifield Road, later changing its name to Kipling Cakes. The site is now home to the Tyre and Exhaust Centre.

Picture credit: Peter Allen

SPECIAL CONSTABLES

This picture belongs to Peter Allen, of Three Bridges, and shows the men who made up Crawley's special constables. The picture is not dated and the only person named is Sir Norman Longley, who can be seen on the left.

*Picture credit:
Peter Allen*

THREE BRIDGES RAILWAY CLUB

This picture shows the members of Three Bridges Railway Club gathered outside the Locomotive Inn. Apart from its name, the Locomotive has not changed much over the years and is instantly recognisable as the Moonraker.

Picture credit: Peter Allen

CRAWLEY FIRE BRIGADE

Sitting on a fire engine in your wedding dress with mud caking your shoes may not be everyone's idea of an ideal start to married life, but this beaming bride was more than happy to be the centre of attention.

These pictures of the men of Crawley Fire Brigade in action belong to Delphine Knight, of West Green. The bride in the picture is her mum, Dorothy Dean, who married firefighter Stan Knight at Ifield Church in 1929.

Ms Knight said that her dad went on to become a sub-officer, while the station officer at the time was Arthur Strevett.

The second picture was taken at Ifield Brook where the crew

Picture credit: Delphine Knight

were called in to rescue a cow, and in the third they are tackling a blaze at the laundry on Leopold Road, West Green – close to the spot where John Haigh would carry out the gruesome 'Acid Bath Murders'.

The final picture shows the funeral procession of John Ernest Ockenden, a Crawley firefighter who retired in 1926 after years of service. Mr Ockenden lived in Croft House, on Ifield Road, and was buried with full Fire Brigade honours.

Picture credit: Delphine Knight

The *Crawley Courier* reported: 'The coffin was carried on the Crawley fire engine which was driven by Engineer SF Stanford. On the front of the engine was a wreath bearing the letters CFB in red carnations on white. The inscription was: "In affectionate remembrance of our Captain and Comrade and a token of sincere appreciation of his 53 years' service in the Brigade – from past and present members of the Crawley Fire Brigade. Well done, good and faithful servant".

'Behind the fire engine came the Crawley tender which was covered with wreaths, and on each side walked firemen.

'At St Peter's Church, members of the Crawley and Horsham Brigades formed a guard of honour through which the coffin was borne by Supts Martin, Bowers, Parsons and Knight, who were in the Brigade with Mr Ockenden.'

THREE BRIDGES BY MRS BETTY ALLEN

Brian Mitchell, of Southgate, found this poem among a collection left by his late mother. He said 'It was written by a Mrs Betty Allen of Three Bridges and it refers to Three Bridges as it was before the new town.'

Field after field of wild flowers and bees,
Long lines of hedgerows, hundreds of trees,
The birds in the Rookery, the sound of the stream,
The haycarts in summer, No! It wasn't a dream.

The milk in a churn, straight from the cow,
Right to your doorstep, I can taste it now!
The Rose Fête at Worth, the fair on the Platt,
The after flood sales, with a sixpenny hat.

The Good Friday sports with egg & spoon races,
Mums' flowery hats, dads sporting braces,
No doctors or bank, no takeaways or 'pop',
Just the butchers, bakers and small village shop.

The flood gates, the hump bridge, over the Mole,
The meadows alive with mice, rabbits and vole,
Caffyns lovely old mill, the Hazelwick Pond,
Could it all come back with the wave of a wand?

The walk to Punch Copse to old Kruger's Den,
That charming old hermit, who shunned fellow men,
Now what's this I see that they call Maidenbower,
Does this mean the demise of pond and wildflower,

The rabbits and squirrels, who lived on Street Hill,
Of green grass and nuts they've all had their fill.
Now they are gone to seek pastures new;
This once lovely sight, now lost to me and you,

I sat on the verge, my head in my hands,
Oh how I miss rolling fields and farmlands.
It's so sad to think, that you of today,
Never knew my old village, in its lovely heyday,

This is your loss, this was my gain,
Could I wake from my dream, and find it's all here
again?

HARRY GANDER

Picture credit: Peter Allen

It is amazing which old pictures published in the *Crawley Observer* have people reaching for the phone to put a name to a face from yesteryear.

School photographs often get little response, but this picture of a little lad and his dog outside a cottage in Ifield in the early 1900s had the phone ringing as soon as the paper hit the shelf and information soon poured in on one of the oldest families in town.

First to call was Pamela Creswick, who said the boy was either her father Harry Gander or his brother Bert and he was standing outside Church Cottages, Ifield Street. And the dog? Well, his name was Toby and he lived to the grand old age of 17!

Mrs Creswick, of Charlwood, said that Harry lived his whole life in Ifield. When he went off to war, she, her mother and sister moved back to the cottage, where her second sister was born in 1940.

She said: 'The toilet was down the garden and the washing was done in a copper in the shed. The kettle was always on. We slept under the stairs on a mattress.

'Mrs Turner lived in the cottage next door and her shed was a little shop. She sold everything! We went to the little school on the corner that is now a cottage.'

Michael Dixon, who is married to Mrs Creswick's cousin Patricia, also named the boy as Harry.

Since his retirement, Mr Dixon and his wife have been researching the related history of the Monk and Gander families and have traced the local line back to George Monk, who was born in between 1630 and 1640. His son, William (1673–1750) moved his family from Bletchingly to Horley before the Monk clan eventually spread down into Ifield – are there any older families than this in the area?

The Monk and Gander families joined when Mrs Dixon's grandmother, Minnie Monk, married William Gander.

THE GANDER FAMILY

The couple are pictured in 1907 with baby Bert and in 1917 with Bert and Harry. Minnie lived in Church Cottages for 70 years. She died in 1971.

HENRY MONK

Henry Monk (1844–1913) – Harry and Bert's grandfather – ran the old Ifield butcher's shop, next to the Plough Inn on Ifield Street and was sexton of St Margaret's Church for 60 years. He was also the parish gravedigger and brewed his own cider.

Picture credit: Michael Dixon

Picture credit: Michael Dixon

Picture credit: Michael Dixon

In an interview with the *Crawley Observer* in 1987, Bert recalled an early memory of pushing young Harry into the churchyard in a wheelbarrow and dumping him in a freshly dug grave!

Bert died in 1988 and Harry in 1998.

ALFRED MONK

The Dixons' research has turned up a host of colourful characters from the Monk/Gander family.

Alfred Monk (1877–1937) was a policeman with the West Sussex force, based at Horsham, and the Dixons managed to track down a photograph of him in full uniform.

George Monk (1881–1950) broke with the family tradition of staying close to home when he emigrated to Canada as a young man.

George's decision to leave the country must have come as a shock to his family. As Mrs Dixon says in

Picture credit: Michael Dixon

her research notes: 'All Minnie Gander's seven grandchildren still live within 10 miles of Ifield Street and most of her great-grandchildren are not too far away either.'

THE SHINDIGS

Forget The Beatles, send the Stones packing – Crawley does not need them – we have got The Shindigs!

In the early 60s these Crawley lads were already busy trying to make their name in the music business – and guitar man Allan Bailey and fellow Shindig Mick Platt still take to the stage today as part of The Soho Leg-ends.

The Shindigs started life as The Daltons and were formed by Allan and his friend Graham Gladwin while the pair were at Hazelwick School.

Graham decided not to stay with the group and the original line up was: Allan (rhythm guitar/vocal), Ken Martin (lead guitar/vocal),

Picture credit: Allan Bailey

Picture credit: Allan Bailey

Andy Page (bass guitar), Brian Redman (drums) and Frank Bennett and Chris Clark (lead vocals). The lead vocals were taken over by Bill Warren and Johnny Ball became drummer.

Allan said, 'We considered ourselves lucky when he defected from The Vincents as John was undoubtedly the finest drummer in the south at the time and was featured at every gig – but sometimes we had to coax him a bit to play a drum solo. His solos were always blistering and stunning.'

Like the legendary Frankie Vaughan, The Daltons had close ties with Crawley Boys' Club and twice represented the club in concert at The Dome, Brighton.

They also played the Royal Festival Hall in a Boys' Clubs battle of the bands. They cut two demos at Tony Pike Music in Putney: an instrumental disc featuring the tracks *Big Noise From Winnetka* and *I Got Rhythm* and a vocal disc featuring *That's My Girl* by Ken Martin and *I'm Coming Home* by Allan Bailey. Mick Platt joined as bass player just before the second disc was recorded.

The band's method of assigning staff was amusing: Ian Page was named manager because he had a sheepskin coat and Sid Sutton was made road manager because he had a van!

The group's big chance came when they appeared on the TV show *Ready, Steady, Win*. They were knocked out in the heats thanks in part to a low vote from Brian Jones of The Rolling Stones.

Picture credit: Allan Bailey

James Cameron joined the group on organ, harmonica and vocals and Andrew J. Wood became manager in 1965.

At his suggestion, The Daltons changed their name to The Shindigs – after an American pop show of the time – and they went on to cut two 45s for Parlophone.

The first featured *One Little Letter* by James Cameron and *What You Gonna Do* by Allan Bailey. The second featured *A Little While Back* and *Why Say Goodbye*, both written by Graham Gouldman, later of 10cc fame.

They performed *A Little While Back* on *Friday Night Spectacular* for Radio Luxembourg and on TV show *The Five O'Clock Club*.

Although they never made it big in the charts, The Shindigs were extremely popular on a local level, with the Gatwick Manor Inn becoming a regular gig.

Allan left the group to pursue a solo singing career including Tony Strudwick, The Trevor Hall Band and The Colin Symons band – even playing before the Queen.

QUEEN'S SILVER JUBILEE

The long, hot summer of 1976 was just a memory when the country got together in 1977 for the biggest party of the decade to mark the Queen's Silver Jubilee.

The streets were awash with red, white and blue, while adults and children alike dressed up and joined in the fun of street parties, fairs and festivals.

Picture credit: Sue Vincent

Sue Vincent, of Tilgate, snapped this picture of the children of Kennet Close, Ifield, who were dolled up in a variety of weird and wonderful costumes for a fancy dress contest.

Sue's son Jamie was four years old at the time and made a very sweet-looking ringmaster – though he did seem more interested in something just out of sight rather than smiling for the camera!

STAGECOACHES

While stagecoaches today are usually only seen on Christmas cards, in Westerns or painted gold to ferry the Queen around on special occasions, they used to be a regular sight in Crawley High Street.

This picture can be seen hanging in the White Hart pub and, after having it cleaned recently, landlord Stuart noticed it included a complete passenger list. It reads: Capt J. Spicer, Capt E.C. Hamilton, Major Stracey, Mr T. Harveyson, Mr T. Tagg, Mr Sid Scarlett, Mr G. Chapman, Mr E.J. Delaforce, Mr T. Halley, Mr P. Harveyson, Mr W. Garrett, Mr E.A. Woodland, Mr E. Fownes, Mr A. Fownes, Mr E.K. Fownes. The picture is dated 23 July 1900.

The Stagecoaches of Great Britain website (*www.anvil.clara.net/stage.htm*) speaks about stagecoach etiquette among passengers: 'It was often said that the real test of a gentleman was his behaviour when a coach stopped on route for the refreshment of its weary passengers.

Picture credit: White Hart, Crawley

'The journey often turned them into starving savages who would descend on the dining room, demanding service.

'The true gentleman would escort a lady from the coach and ensure she was provided with dinner and pay her bill. This inevitably meant that it was impossible for him to eat himself, as time was strictly limited. The inn-keepers would often exacerbate the situation by delaying the food so passengers had little time to eat their fill before they had to be on the road again.'

It certainly paid to be a member of the fairer sex in those days!

PLACES

THE SUN

Anyone who has lived in Crawley for any length of time will have heard the old joke about the town having the longest road known to man – it stretched from the sun to the moon. Or the Sun to the Half Moon, if we want to be accurate.

No matter how much Crawley changes – from village to new town and so on

Picture credit: Tony Syrett

– its pubs remain faithful reminders of the past. In the town centre alone you are never more than a stone's throw from one of the historic watering holes – and they all have tales to tell.

While most of them have hardly changed over the years, the Sun is long gone – having made way for the bustling Leisure Park.

Picture credit: Tony Syrett

THE BREWERY SHADES

Crawley residents who were around before the new town will remember when the Brewery Shades pub was extended.

These pictures belong to Pam Hayes, whose parents Kenneth and Lily Ferns ran the pub from 1953. Mr Ferns died at the age of 61 just short of his retirement. Mrs Ferns passed away in 2006 at the age of 91.

The first picture was taken in 1953 during the extension of what would be the pub's off-licence, while the one below is obviously much older.

Picture credit: Pam Hayes

Pam was 17 when the family moved into the flat above the pub and she lived there until she married at the age of 20. She said, 'I used to go down and play darts in the bar but I wasn't allowed to serve customers.'

Pam eventually went to work at Rosina's in the Broadwalk, which sold ladies' clothes and underwear. Once the off-licence opened for business, she went to work there.

Pam remembers being spooked by the pub's resident ghost: 'I never saw it but I used to hear doors closing when there was no one there. It could be a bit scary upstairs on your own.'

Picture credit: Pam Hayes

COLIN EDGAR

This fascinating bunch of pictures are from the collection of Colin Edgar, of Southgate.

The snowy picture was taken in the High Street near the Brewery Shades. The local milkman can be seen steering his horse and cart past the Shades in 1928 in the photograph on the right.

The little tree to his right is the Crawley Oak, which now towers over the pub.

Picture credit: Colin Edgar   *Picture credit: Colin Edgar*

This picture with the Yetman & Sons butcher's van is a High Street shot. The large house in the background is the Temperance House. Bar Med now stands on that spot and Mr Edgar wondered what the clean-living Temperance folk would make of the change.

Picture credit: Colin Edgar

Picture credit: Colin Edgar   *Picture credit: Colin Edgar*

This shot shows the horse fair in 1923. The gate is across the entrance to Bank Lane looking towards what is now Barclays Bank on the High Street.

The picture above was taken at the beginning of the 20th century and shows the old post office. At first glance the 'ER' carved above the door looks odd given the date, but suggests the building was dedicated to King Edward VII.

STATION ROAD

Crawley lost a vital font of historical knowledge when teacher Roger Bastable died. A Crawley man through and through, his enthusiasm for local history certainly seemed to rub off on at least one of his friends.

These pictures belong to Steve Stenning – and he showed them to Roger before his death. He said, 'I am proud that I knew Roger as a friend. His work on the Crawley

Picture credit: Steve Stenning

Picture credit: Steve Stenning

History pages in the *Crawley Observer* was so interesting. I have all of Roger's publications, signed by Roger himself, and I find them so inspirational regarding Crawley's history.

'Some time ago, just before Roger's illness, I came across an historic picture that I had not seen before while enjoying a pint in my local club with friends. It was a picture of a street with the St John's tower in the background. Myself and my friends were curious about where the picture was taken from. As you can imagine, one or two friendly arguments occurred as to who was right.

'So to prove the point, armed with my camera, I decided to track down the exact spot where the picture was taken. It turned out to be taken from the station end of Station Road. I took a photograph of Station Road from what I believe was the same spot as the original. Rather proud of my achievement, I gave the before and after photographs to Roger. He was so fascinated by this approach that he said he would publish them in the *Observer*.

'Sadly, before he could, his illness took over and he stopped the work he used to do for the *Observer*. I am therefore wondering, as a tribute to Roger, whether these photographs could now be published as Roger intended.'

Linda Shouler remembers her mother telling her about the strange-looking tree on the right of the old picture. She said, 'The tree used to fascinate me. My mum told me it was a monkey puzzle tree and if I remember rightly it was in or near the garden of Crawley police station.'

Gwendoline Pain said: 'My granny and granddad lived at No.25 Station Road, right next door to the police station. The monkey puzzle tree was further up the road [towards the railway line].

'Number 25 is the house on the left of the police station. They lived there until my granny died on Christmas Day 1970, aged 90. Their names were William and Charlotte Ford.'

OLD CRAWLEY POLICE STATION

Peter Allen provided this picture of the old Crawley Police Station, which shows Sgt Thomas Martin with his wife and children outside the building.

Mr Allen, of Three Bridges, said, 'I don't know the exact date of the picture, but I know that in those days, the Sergeant and his family would have lived in the building.'

Picture credit: Peter Allen

HANDY CORNER SHOP

This picture belongs to Sheila White, of Langley Green, and shows the Handy Corner shop, at 18 Springfield Road. Mrs White said, 'My husband's parents were bombed out of Croydon during the war and came to Crawley and opened the shop. Their names were Lilly and Edward Small and they moved to Horsham.'

Mrs White added that notorious Acid Bath Murderer, John George Haigh, frequented the shop to buy his cigarettes.

She believes the shop later became a video store.

Picture credit: Shelia White

CRAWLEY HOSPITAL

Can you guess what it is yet? The sun was certainly shining on these young builders as they built a much-needed hospital for the new towners of Crawley.

These pictures belong to Loretta Walsh, whose father was part of the crew to construct the West Green Drive hospital. They were taken around 1963 but Loretta does not have an exact date.

Picture credit: Loretta Walsh

Picture credit: Loretta Walsh

Looking at the top picture, health and safety rules appear to have been a lot more lax in the 1960s than they are today – not a hard hat or safety jacket in sight!

However they went about their work, the builders did a good job – and it certainly took the pressure off of Crawley's tiny cottage hospital.

Picture credit: Loretta Walsh

Picture credit: *Loretta Walsh*

Picture credit: *Loretta Walsh*

THE WHITE KNIGHT

The White Knight was 50 years old in 2007. Landlords Bridget and John Brant had been pulling pints at the pub for three years and were determined to make sure its history did not become the stuff of long-forgotten memory. The Brants did a little digging and came up with some gems of information about the pub.

The name, for instance, makes many people think of the legend of St George, but an old picture of a huge wall-mounted chess board that used to stand at the entrance to the bar indicated an *Alice Through The Looking Glass* connection. A very old copy of the *Crawley Observer* bore this out when its description of the pub's opening day included 'framed blow-ups of original illustrations from the book'.

One customer told John that she remembered workmen pulling down the board during renovation work, but she could not recall when that was.

The popular local has certainly seen some changes down the years. Old customers will remember a couple of bowling lanes standing where the dance floor is now. And those who have enjoyed a pint or two there since it first opened will remember the glass wall that used to make it clear to all what everyone had in their glasses.

The *Crawley Observer* from Friday 4 October 1957, reported, 'One idea that goes by the board in the design of the White Knight is that drinking is a secret occupation. The walls of both the saloon and public bars fronting onto the paved terrace are made also entirely of glass.'

Like the chess board and the bowling alley, though, the wall is long gone.

John discovered that the old pub sign used to depict a white knight chess piece and the Brants ordered a brand new sign bearing the same design.

The first landlord and landlady were Peggy and Bert Hammond and a little café used to stand at the front of the pub.

CRAWLEY MARKET

This picture shows Crawley Market and is dated May 1905.

Over the years, the market has moved back and forth from the High Street, spending a period of time on Orchard Street at the site that became the car park.

COUNTY MALL

It is hard to imagine Crawley without County Mall, and this selection of pictures from the *Observer* archive shows the 'before', 'during' and 'after' of the Mall, including a couple of memorable 'visitors' who occupied the shop floor.

The Mall was opened in April 1992 by Mayor Bill Pye. As with all major development projects, the people of Crawley had had to live with months of inconvenience as a large chunk of their town centre turned into a building site.

Before the Mall was built, the site was used as a car park and bus station and, when Crawley held a carnival parade, the floats could meet there, ready for the off.

Shopping can be extremely dull for children, but the Mall was never short of an attraction or two to keep little minds occupied.

Pictured right is Keith Bridges with the County Mall dinosaur in 1993, while above is Terry the Singing Tree pictured with children from Northgate Middle School.

QUEENS SQUARE

Do you remember when Tesco and a fountain depicting a boy on a dolphin dominated Queens Square, or when a road ran through the square itself?

These pictures were donated by William Godfrey, of Langley Green, and are an example of how much the town centre has changed over the last few decades.

Picture credit: William Godfrey

Picture credit: William Godfrey

THE BROAD WALK

This picture shows the Broad Walk as it was in its heyday, bustling with shoppers and not a To Let sign in sight.

ST MARY'S CHURCH

While the new town celebrated its 60th anniversary, one of its churches marked its 50th.

St Mary's Church, in Southgate, was the first Parish Church to be built in Sussex after World War Two. Three others have been built in Crawley since 1958 – St Andrew's, Furnace Green; Christ the Lord, Broadfield; and Holy Trinity, Tilgate.

These pictures were donated by Curate Kevin Lewis, who worked alongside the Rector Revd Tim Wilson in 2008 at the Wakehurst Drive Church.

This picture is from the *Observer* dated 31 January 1958 and shows Dr G.K.A. Bell, Bishop of Chichester, who, in his last official engagement before retiring, consecrated the church. He is chatting with Revd Gerald Bridgeman, the first Rector, who joined the church in 1956 – two years before the building was finished.

In his account of the history of St Mary's, Revd Bridgeman recalled his decision to move from Oxford to start a new life in a town that was little more than a building site. He said, 'We were among the first arrivals in the neighbourhood and our only "neighbours" were the shells of the half-completed houses around us. There were no street lights and everything seemed very primitive.

'Our first main task was to find a place in which to hold services. The only possible building seemed to be a large, bleak-looking workmen's canteen in which the Sunday school organiser for the new town had been holding a small children's class for a few weeks.

'It was the end of October and very cold and so we looked for a smaller building which we would be able to heat.

'Adjoining the canteen was a smaller one, used by the foremen. The building contractors kindly allowed us the use of it and one of their men offered to light a fire each Sunday in the old stove.

'Our first services on 4 November 1956 were attended by a total of 33 grown-ups and children. Although, on occasions, they were nearly choked by the fumes from the stove, the faithful few came along week by week. The building was very crude and rough-shod but it had been a stable and we could not help remembering that Christ was born in a similar building, and it was not inappropriate that the church in Southgate should have come to life in a stable-canteen.'

Ron Wilkinson, of Furnace Green, was one of the builders who gave the church its distinctive look. He and his wife moved from Dulwich, London, after Ron had spent 20 months helping build houses in Crawley. He said, 'At that time work became short, and I saw the church just rising from the foundations. The builders were Bishop & Clark from Horley, as I remember, so I called into the site office and they gave me a job as a shuttering hand – that is a carpenter making the moulds out of very sturdy wood to form the very complicated shapes the church required.

'The whole of the concrete shapes in the church were created by carpenters. We created the wooden mould shapes and in went the steel reinforcing followed by concrete – which was mixed on site and wheelbarrowed to the particular mould being filled. Gradually the church began to rise from the oversite. There was masses of scaffolding inside and outside the church for the men to work on and support the moulds and to take all that weight of steel and concrete until it all set.

'The main concrete beams holding the roof went from one side of the church to the other and had to be continuously poured with concrete until they were full. Carpenters had to stand by just in case the shuttering [mould] moved. It was a tense time – tons of steel and concrete.

'Finally the belfry went on top of that previous work, once again made from concrete, and, I might add, it was very cold and windy. I can remember we had fires alight in oil drums just to try and keep warm.

'For a bit of fun we made a television aerial out of wood and stuck it on the top of the belfry – we got into trouble for that and had to take it down!

'The altar wall – which is also in concrete and a very complicated piece of moulding, was undertaken by special carpenters as the church progressed. The coloured glass inserts were added at a later date.

'During the time I was working on the site our first son was growing up so I took advantage of the woodworking shop we had in the church and made him a play pen in my own time – with the site manager's permission, of course! This was very successful and was used for his brothers and sister as well.

'I didn't stay to work on any of the internal woodwork. When I pass the church it brings back memories of my working life in Crawley. Our second son, who now lives in Australia, was christened in the church. I only wish we took a photograph.

'This story is as a result of me calling into the church about a month ago to one of their coffee mornings and looking round the church that I have not been in for about 48 years – how time flies.'

St Mary's Church was one of the stop-off points for the Queen during her 1958 visit to the town – and the people of Southgate certainly gave her an enthusiastic welcome.

Under the headline 'Crowd cheered ice cream van!' the *Crawley Courier* reported on 13 June 1958: 'How the car managed to drive up to the entrance of St Mary's Church remains a mystery. Even more skilful was the expert way the driver manoeuvred his vehicle away after the visit without knocking half a dozen people over. For on both occasions the royal couple were mobbed by their cheering subjects. Even the score of policemen there couldn't stop them.

'The puny wire fencing that surrounded the grounds of the church did not hold the crowd for long, and as soon as Her Majesty and Prince Philip had entered the church, they swept across to crowd around the doorway and wait for her return.

'While waiting for the royal visitors to arrive, the restless onlookers cheered everything that passed, including a busload of policemen and a small ice cream van.'

The Queen may not have been present when the church marked its 50th anniversary, but it was certainly a celebration to remember.

Three of the previous four rectors – Revd Gerald Bridgeman, Revd Terry Fuller and Revd Alan Hawker – returned to the church, while Revd Jonathan Mortimer, who was unable to attend, sent his best wishes. Curate Kevin Lewis said, 'Over 430 people came – the biggest service for at least 20 years, with every chair in the church used.'

The Rector, Revd Tim Wilson, preached on how the vision of the church is to look forward, building on the tremendous foundations of the last 50 years and looking forward to the next 50.

He talked about how, although they were celebrating the 50th anniversary of the building, the church is not the building but the people in it.

Fifty helium-filled gold balloons were released by the children during one of the songs and there was cake for all.

What better way to seal bonds of friendship than with a holiday? In September 1959 the parishioners from St Mary's Church headed off to Mabledon Park, Tonbridge. They are seen here next to their bus (right). The parishioners travelled to Shanklin, on the Isle of Wight, in 1976. Top right in the picture is Roy Sumpter, who organised the trip.

CRAWLEY HIGH STREET

Crawley High Street really has not changed much over the years, as these pictures from the 1920s show. They belong to Pete Allen, of Three Bridges, who had them reproduced from glass negatives. Despite the age of the images they are remarkably clear and show the area of the High Street that is now Grand Parade. The Central Garage Motor Engineers stood roughly where the Jubilee Oak pub is today. Mr Allen says that the Lindfield's Garage (pictured overleaf) is the same garage as that on the right of the picture below.

David Harman, who lives in Hailsham, says the people marching in the road waving a banner are members of the Ancient Order of Foresters: 'I've got quite close connections with the society and I've been doing a bit of research into the history.

Picture credit: Peter Allen

'There is no branch in Crawley now. They joined with Horley 20 years ago and are now with Horsham.'

According to its website (*www.foresters.ws/index*), the Ancient Order of Foresters was formed in 1834, though its origins lie in a much older society called the Royal Foresters, which was formed in the 18th century. The website continued: 'This seems at first to have been a purely sociable society until the members decided that they had a duty to assist their fellow men who fell into need "as they walked through the forests of life". This "need" arose principally when a breadwinner fell ill, could not work and, therefore, received no wages.

'Illness and death left families financially distressed and often destitute. Relief of this need has been the main purpose of the Foresters throughout their long history. It was achieved by members paying, initially, a few pence a week into a common fund from which sick pay and funeral grants could be drawn.'

OLD CRAWLEY STATION

The view below will be instantly recognisable to original Crawley folk and new towners, but may be something of a mystery to anyone who was not here before the 1970s. The picture was sent in by Pete Allen and shows the first Crawley Railway Station.

The station, which stood near the Railway Pub and level crossing, was built in February 1848 and closed in July 1968 in favour of the current building a few yards along the track.

At the right of the picture we can see the pub and its ballroom – which was gutted by fire in the 1960s. Note the adverts for Oxo and Walls!

The picture is guaranteed to spark memories for Peter Barton, of Ifield, who remembers that there used to be a railway-run rent office near the station. The rent was collected from houses on Ifield Road, near Snell Hatch Cemetery, which were owned by the railway. He said, 'There were about 10 houses and they all had green doors. The rent was 10 shillings and sixpence.'

As a lad, Mr Barton was given the job of taking his grandfather's weekly rent to the rent offices – his reward for which was a sweet. His grandfather, Sidney Ellis, lived at number 139.

Mr Barton said: 'I used to run up with my rent book and the rent. I remember going through the fence and they would always write out the receipt by hand.'

Picture credit: Peter Allen

CYCLISTS

Cyclists congregating outside Ifield Post Office.

Picture credit: Peter Allen

HORSE AND CART

A horse and trap at Oak Tree Farm.

Picture credit: Peter Allen

IFIELD STORE

Children playing in the road outside Ifield Store – undated but the picture indicates that the roof had recently undergone repair.

Picture credit: Peter Allen

THE PLOUGH

It is surprising how little the older parts of Ifield have changed over the years. This picture shows a view of the Plough public house, although who the gentleman relaxing outside is we have no idea.

Picture credit: Peter Allen

This is the view past the Plough down to the church.

Picture credit: Peter Allen

ROYAL OAK

This gang of men and boys were gathered outside the Royal Oak pub.

Picture credit: Peter Allen

IFIELD SCHOOL

These girls were taking a break from lessons in the playground at Ifield School. The picture was taken in around 1910 and they certainly seem to have been a well-behaved bunch!

Ifield School. AB1

Picture credit: Peter Allen

1950s HIGH STREET

This delightful snapshot of the High Street was taken in the 1950s from close to the – much smaller – Jubilee Oak tree.

The picture comes from the collection of Pete Allen, from Three Bridges, and, although instantly recognisable, it shows how much the High Street has changed over the years.

Margaret Delasalles, of Broadfield, and her mother Sheila Hall have proved to be a fount of information when it comes to the shops which used to trade in the High Street. Mrs Delasalles, who has always lived in Crawley, said, 'There were a lot of little shops along there. There was an old haberdasher called Smith's Clothing Company. They used to sell the old nylon overalls. I'm sure it was a double-fronted shop.

'There was a camera shop in the middle of the High Street and mum was saying she can remember Fludes on the corner of Robinson Road. Before that it could have been an antiques shop. There was also a Mences hardware shop.'

Mrs Delasalles remembers walking to work at Battens Bakery in the 1960s and 70s 'before they knocked it down'.

She remembers Warren's Hardware on the corner of Ifield Road and Freeman Hardy Willis in the 70s.

Picture credit: Peter Allen

If you want to find out about the history of a town, the best people to ask are those who have lived there the longest. Mary Mitchell's father Stanley Burr is surely a contender for having lived in Crawley the longest. She said, 'Other than war service, he has lived in Crawley since 1914. He is a great local historian and says he remembers all the shops in the High Street.'

Mrs Mitchell's late mother was also Crawley born and bred – her father was Job Freeman, who founded the local builders J. Freeman and sons. Mrs Mitchell, who was born in 1948, said, 'For many years the company had the contract to maintain the houses belonging to the New Towns Commission, but the firm folded when the last of the son's generation died. Many of the next generation still live in the town.'

Regarding the High Street, Mr Burr recalled, 'Starting from the level crossing gates the shop that is now the Taj Mahal was for many years previously a hairdresser's called Simmonds, but before that it was a café run by two brothers called Newport.

'Each brother had a son and the two cousins each had a Morris van, which they used to deliver bread and cakes around the area. The two cousins used to race each other up and down the Brighton Road in the vans.

'The cafe did good business with people arriving by train, as this was the original site of the railway station. Next to that was the entrance to a yard, which became known as Hammer Yard because there had been a blacksmith there.

'On the other side was a shop which I had known as Phyllis Braden's. Miss Braden ran the shop herself and sold sewing and knitting materials. Prior to that it was a butcher's called Burtons. Burtons also had a shop in Horsham. The next shop was White's which was an outfitters'. Whites employed their own seamstresses and ladies wishing to buy a dress would go in and choose the pattern and the fabric and the seamstresses would make the dress up.

'The shop on the corner of Robinson Road was previously a second-hand furniture shop, but prior to that it was a gents outfitters' called Pace's.'

Mrs Mitchell picked up the thread from her memories of the 1950s onwards: 'If you moved down from White's there was a tobacconist and sweet shop called Kale's. They also had another smaller shop on the other side near to Iceland. The shop sold tobacco loose from jars and the smell was wonderful.

'Next to that I think was a large imposing building which was the Westminster Bank, later to become the National Westminster when it amalgamated with the National Provincial Bank. Then there was a gap which may have been a house and then the Batten's. It was a really good baker and they also had a shop at Three Bridges. I vaguely remember that it was a grocer's shop before that and that my mother used to buy bacon which was sliced off the side of the pig to order.

'The hardware shop referred to was actually called Mence Smith's. It always had piles of goods for sale on the pavement outside the shop.

'Other shops I remember were the Co-op and the Co-op butcher, which were further down, more or less opposite the entrance to St John's and, of course, Bastable's fish shop. They always had fresh fish on a cold slab but also lots of chickens and game hanging up across the front of the shop.

'Further down, in Grand Parade, was Woolworths. It had polished wooden floors and each department had its own high counter. There was no self-service or check-outs so you had to go from counter to counter waiting to be served and paying as you went. Next to that was an undertaker which I think may have been Bartley and Ward. The Crawley Market was more or less built on the site of my aunt and uncle's house and Orchard Street was built on their orchard.

'My uncle was a tailor and worked for his father in a tiny shop called Camfield's. I remember that they had huge bolts of fabric which you had to go and choose and have made up for you. The Camfields were prominent members of the Society of Friends [Quakers] at Ifield and I believe my uncle, Eric Camfield, also served as a reserve firefighter. Opposite Camfield's on the corner next to what is now the Rat and Parrot was a shoe shop and repairers called Tompsetts. Mr Tompsett lived in Oak Road in Southgate and his garden backed on to ours in Springfield Road.

'Further along next to the White Hart was a greengrocer called Hemsley's. They sold seeds as well as fruit and veg. The seed was loose and was sold by the ounce and stored in wooden drawers. I remember my father buying half an ounce of carrot seeds, which were weighed out and then put into a little paper bag which was labelled by hand.

'Mr Hemsley was called Jack and was a tall, thin man. His wife was quite a large lady and I remember her cooking beetroot in the shop in a huge pan rather like a cannibal's pot.

'Hemsley's also had a shop at Pease Pottage opposite the Grapes, and this one had a large market garden behind it. Next to Hemsley's was a café and cake shop called Reynold's Café. My mother used to take me there for lunch sometimes. The cake shop was at the front and the cafe at the rear. They used to sell coffee-flavour ice cream, which I loved and still retain a passion for to this day. At the end of this block was Mrs Crowe's art shop, which was a real treasure trove. She was a nice lady who once helped me find a kitten when I was wanting to home one.

'Along by Iceland was Kales' other shop, but also the original site of the Trustee Savings Bank, where my sister used to work. She had to keep all the records by hand and add everything up herself at the end of the day without even an adding machine.

'Then there was a shop called Penfold's, which sold garden materials and pet food. It also sold tropical fish, which were always kept in the window. Then there was the opening into Three Bridges Road, which was later renamed Haslett Avenue. On the other side was the Post Office on the site that is now the Barclaycard offices. The original Post Office, though, had been in Robinson Road, which was previously called Post Office Road. When I was a child this had become a glove factory.

'Moving further up towards the crossing gates there was a stationers', which I think may have been called Willett's, and then a chemist shop called Sadlers.

'There was another chemist further up in Brighton Road called Crombies. The Crombies had twin daughters and my uncle married one of them. The other one continued to run the shop with her brother for many years. The business later combined with Sadlers and traded as Crombie and Sadler. A chemist still trades under this name on the corner of East Park, although I do not think there is any connection to the family now.

'Beyond the level crossing there was a baker called Skinners next to the Railway Hotel and a grocers shop on the corner of East Park called Garretts. Opposite the site which became occupied by the Peugeot dealer had been the Imperial Cinema, and it still bears the name. It was operated as a cinema for many years, although the original cinema in the town had been a corrugated iron building in East Park.

'When I was a child the cinema was the Embassy, which is now called Bar Med, and the Imperial was used as an auction salesroom.

'Next door was a garage and then an estate agent called Wood Son and Gardener. They always fascinated me because their telephone number was Crawley 1.'

Stella Slight, from Horley, was born in Crawley and told the tale of how the distance from the Sun pub to the Half Moon was always said to be a mile.

She said, 'On the left-hand side of the street, opposite the Sun, was the entrance to Woolborough Road where I was born in 1939. On the corner was a sort of scrapyard and a house that was owned by the Holmes family, then a row of about 12 cottages. I can remember the end one being a small general store at one time.

'Next came two more houses before the bus station on the corner of Northgate Road. On the other corner of Northgate Road was Boxall & Collins Garage, then a small factory before the laundry and Northgate Café.

'There was a lovely old house (the front of it is still incorporated in the newer buildings there now). Then came a double-fronted detached house. I can remember that a lady lived there once who owned a smallholding on the opposite side of the road that went back behind the Sun and the old bowling club. My dad used to run it for her back in the 1940s.

'I can remember the beautiful house called The Tree as it used to be. There used to be a lodge at the entrance of the drive leading up to the Rectory [now the Boulevard].'

THE PUNCH BOWL

'The Punch Bowl still stands, looking much as it did years ago. There used to be greens all along the edge of the road with bench seats for everyone to enjoy.

'I can remember in the 1950s all the teenagers used to congregate on these sort of lawns as there was very little to do in Crawley in those days. From the Punch Bowl there was a row of cottages and then a small garage with two petrol pumps outside.

'Then came two small shops, one a shoe shop and the other one a greengrocer shop, and I can remember a sweet shop standing there before the White Hart pub. The shops started with a greengrocer

run by Mr Hemsley, then Reynolds café and cake shop, a grocery shop, an art shop, Army & Navy Stores and a radio shop (owned by my uncle Sid Withers).'

THE ANCIENT PRIORS

'Then came the Ancient Priors, which has had many different tenants over the years. In the next block of shops was Kingham's Grocers before Church Walk. After Church Walk came a ladies' dress shop at

Picture credit: Gordon Seeking

one time and one other shop before the entrance to St John's Church. The next block of shops consisted of Clarke's cake shop, Kales tobacco shop, another small shoe shop and Smith's men's clothing store before the turning into Three Bridges Road.

'I think there was Wilkins Butchers on the other side, then a dress shop and Muhallands Shoe Shop and a book shop. The old Post Office was originally on this side of the road and Willetts Stationery Shop.'

WITHERS RADIO AND TELEVISION SERVICE

'In 1955 my uncle moved from down the street and opened up a larger radio and television shop which I used to work in on a Saturday. I know Crombies the Chemist was on the corner of Station Road. They were also in the Brighton Road at some time. The other corner of Station Road was the Cabin and then the entrance to the railway station. After the station and level crossing is Brighton Road and the Railway Hotel where there were always Saturday night dances.

'I can remember the first coffee bar opening in the basement of the bakers in the next block of shops. This was really something great to happen for the teenagers in the early 1950s.

'After the entrance to East Park there were a few more shops before you came upon the lovely houses leading up to the Half Moon pub. Coming back north from the Half Moon were a lot more nice houses, including Ravendean, the doctors' surgery. Further down was the Imperial Cinema, where my dad was

the manager back in the 30s, and then the garage. Up behind the garage was a small road with four terraced houses, known as Bank Terrace – my grandparents lived there. This was also an entrance for Stanley Ball's off-licence.

'On the corner of Springfield Road was a bank – Nightingale House. The other side of Springfield Road was the railway line and level crossing. At one time there were steps going down to a small tunnel to take you under the railway lines to the other side into the High Street.

'There were a couple of shops where the Taj Mahal Indian restaurant opened. A yard went around the back of the shops before you came to more shops and another great building which could have been a bank or solicitors (long gone though). I can remember the next place was an employment agency (I went there for my first job). I know the International Stores was along this side of the street before you came to Robinson Road.

'After Robinson Road came a few more shops, including a small ladies' shop, the ironmongery run by the Warren sisters and Bastables. I also think there was a gas or electricity showroom along there before you came to Miss Smith's drapery store and Freeman Hardy Willis shoe shop on the corner of Ifield Road.

'Before the George Hotel there were a couple of shops. After the George came a florists and among that parade of shops was Bellman's Wool Shop and Woolworths. After the cinema came fields and another green on the side of the street. I can remember a rather large house which I believe was run as some sort of guest house, before you came to more fields until you reached the Sun pub.

'Next to the Sun was a small grocery shop that was run by Mr and Mrs Dorkings, then a couple of cottages before the bowling green club. Stoners builders was on the opposite of the street.'

YETMAN'S BUTCHERS SHOP

David Baker donated this picture of Yetman's butcher shop on behalf of Mrs Thrift – a relative of the Yetmans. He said the shop used to stand in the High Street.

Picture credit: Mrs Thrift

IFIELD STEAM MILL

(With thanks to the Ifield Village Conservation Area Advisory Committee and Crawley Museum Society.) Did you know that there is a corner of Berlin that will be forever Ifield – at least as long as the Verkehr und Technik Museum is standing? The museum is home to the steam engine that used to be housed in the Ifield Steam Mill, having been given it on long-term loan by the Science Museum. In a letter to the Crawley Museum Society from the Science Museum, the Wolf Compound Engine is described as 'the only engine of this type and age that we have in the collection'.

In 2000, the Ifield Village Conservation Area Advisory Committee (IVCAAC) compiled a history of the Mill – and it makes for fascinating reading.

In 1834, Lord Rodney, the lord of the manor, gave the site and the windmill to the miller in acknowledgement of his service to Ifield. In 1837, the *Court Book of Ifield Manor* recorded that on 29 May 1837 the lords of the manor assigned a parcel of land on Ifield Green to James Bristow (described as farmer and miller, resident at Ifield Court) 'on which the said James Bristow hath lately erected and built a windmill'.

In 1839 the windmill within Ifield Green was shown on the Tithe Map. James Bristow was recorded as being the owner and occupier of the windmill and land and owner of the cottage and land on Langley Lane. Timothy Avery was recorded as the occupier.

Picture credit: Crawley Museum

On 2 January 1855, an addition was made to the *Court Book* entry which read 'whereas the said James Bristow hath since erected another mill, being a steam flour mill upon the said premises'.

The steam mill is shown on a new map in 1855, which therefore dates its addition to between 1841 and 1855. The IVCAAC reasons that, given that the new steam mill roof was made of slate, which is likely to have originated from North Wales, it was probably constructed in the early 1850s. The material was not widely available in south-east England until the rail network was in place – and the lines to Three Bridges and Crawley opened in 1841 and 1848 respectively.

Though the precise date that the steam engine and boiler were installed is unclear, the *Sussex Advertiser of Lewes* and *Brighthelmstone Journal* of 22 June 1835 stated that a steam engine of similar specification was auctioned by the owners of Ifield Water Corn Mill on 29 June 1835. It is possible that James Bristow purchased it and stored it until he could afford to build the steam mill.

An additional clue to its construction date is recorded in the *Model Engineer and Light Machinery Review*, dated 13 September 1928, when A.G. Paige RN, a retired warrant officer engineer who lived in Ifield Park, reported that the compound condensing beam engine looked like being scrapped and hoped a home could be found for it. Paige said that the engine had been installed 72 years previously, suggesting a date of 1856. In the edition of 18 October 1928 he said, 'Mr Warren, a retired builder in Ifield, helped to put the engine and boiler in and he also helped me on Saturday last to hoist the beam out'.

Stephen Warren was 86 in 1928 and would have been 14 in 1856. It is clear that the steam mill on Ifield Green was in regular use from no later than 1860. The IVCAAC compilation reads: 'The installation and use of the steam engine demanded a ready supply of cooling water. This was achieved from a well under the engine, 30 metres deep, and three outlying wells, with hot water circulating between them for cooling before returning to the principal well.

'The women folk of the village used to catch the hot water as it ran from the mill on its cooling circuit for their regular weekly laundry. It seems likely that the outlying wells were near the pond, about 50 metres south of the mill, which was reputed by old Ifield inhabitants to have held cooling water. These wells would have been excavated before the engine was installed.'

Picture credit: Crawley Museum

Don Warren, Stephen Warren's great-grandson, was told by his parents that Stephen built the Royal Oak and that he dug the ironstone used in the front elevation from pits on Ifield Green. There is no evidence that there ever were adequate quarrying pits on Ifield Green, suggesting that the 'pits' were in fact the wells for the steam mill and that young Stephen may have had a hand in the excavation.

The Science Museum inventory of 1914 states that the flour mill was in use until 1914. In the 1950s the mill and its lands were purchased as a probate sale by the Development Corporation during the early 1950s in order to preserve it. Ownership was passed to Crawley Council in 1956 and from 1959 it housed one of the Crawley units of the Nautical Training Corps – T.S. *Courageous*.

Picture credit: Crawley Museum

The boiler chimney at the north end of the steam mill and the pond, which supplied the cooling water for the condenser, were in situ until about 1960. Soon afterwards the chimney was declared unsafe and demolished and the pond was condemned as a danger to children and filled in, no doubt with the rubble from the chimney.

In the 1980s the NTC left because, without external financial support, they found the cost of maintenance was too great for them to bear.

Plans to turn the mill into a craft centre were halted after the council called in the lease, claiming the tenant was not fulfilling repair and maintenance requirements.

The mill – which is unique as the only early Victorian industrial building in Crawley – was boarded up for two years until a fire on 10 January 2000 seriously damaged the slate roof and timbers.

IFIELD WATERMILL

(With thanks to Nick and Angela Sexton and Crawley Museum Society.)

The millers who worked Ifield Watermill are long since gone, but one of their descendants paid a recent visit to the mill and helped fill in a little family history. Susanne Brooker provided Crawley Museum Society with information about her great-grandfather Richard Harding, the first of the Harding family to run the mill, initially as a tenant and later as the owner. Her grandfather, Arthur Harding, spent his boyhood at the mill. He helped his father and brothers run the mill before, during and after World War One. Richard was born in 1829 in Linchmere, Sussex.

Susanne said that her great-grandfather was a miller 'foreman' at Stokes Mill, Burpham, East Sussex. He married Lois Baker in about 1861, and they had William and George. Susanne wrote, 'In 1874 Richard and family moved to Ifield and became tenants at the mill in 1881, living at the Mill House. William, George and Arthur worked for their father in the mill. The family now included Ernest, Amy, Alice, Elizabeth and Charles.

'Alice and Elizabeth were born at the Mill House, and in about 1885 Richard became the owner of Ifield Mill. Although the original Mill was built in 1684, the building Richard knew was built in 1817 for £3,500. In 1891, Richard and his son Ernest are recorded as the millers. Charles was carter at the mill but died in 1915, probably in World War One.

'The Hardings ran the mill until about 1925. Richard Harding died in 1927 and his wife Lois in 1919. They are buried in Rudgwick. My grandfather was Arthur Harding, one of Richard Harding's sons. Arthur did not go into the milling business, as his brothers did. He became a tailor. Arthur had a tailoring shop in Lesborne Road, Reigate, Surrey.

Picture credit: Crawley Museum

'He married Suzanna Comber in 1889. They had eight children, Stanley, Winnie, Susie (my mother born in 1891), Lois (known as Dorothy), Charles, Maurice, Gladys, Richard and Faith.'

Susanne remembers her grandfather with great affection. She described him as tall, distinguished, with white curly hair. He became very forgetful. He often spoke of the mill and swimming across the mill pond as a young man. Arthur died in about 1945 in his 80s. His wife Suzan died in the early 1930s. Stanley, their eldest son, was killed in World War One at Loos.

Winnie (Susanne's mother) married William Roberts in 1919 and went to live in North Wales. Their children are Stanley, Winifred, Pamela, Mair and Susanne. Susanne said that family folklore has it that one of Richard Harding's sons emigrated to the US.

At the end of her visit, Susanne presented the mill with a Harding christening gown. She said that the gown had been the christening gown for several members of the family. It will be displayed on mill opening days and Museum Society members plan to prepare and display Susanne's family tree in more detail at the mill.

IFIELD ROUNDABOUT

The picture below belongs to Rex Williams, of Turners Hill, and was created using two snapshots. It shows some wonderful old vehicles navigating the Ifield roundabout. Mr Williams said, 'When Crawley bypass was built [now called Crawley Avenue] a roundabout had to be constructed where it crossed over the Crawley to Ifield road. A pair of council houses was demolished on the eastern side of Ifield Road, numbers 263 and 261.'

Picture credit: Rex Williams

ROYAL VISITORS

QUEEN ELIZABETH II

The English have always loved a bit of pomp and circumstance – it is one of the things we do best – and in 1958 the people of Crawley took to the streets to welcome Queen Elizabeth II to the new town. The bustling new town – one of eight created after World War Two to take the strain off of an overcrowded London – played fine host to the vibrant young monarch still in the first decade of her reign.

The Queen was accompanied by her husband the Duke of Edinburgh – who managed to avoid making any of his now legendary verbal faux pas (or if he didn't, they were kept very quiet).

The royal couple visited Three Bridges School and Crawley College. Her Majesty planted a tree in Queens Square and, surrounded by crowds of happy new towners, they strolled along the Broad Walk and took lunch in the George.

They passed within the shadow of the beautiful Jubilee Oak tree, which was planted in around 1887 to mark the diamond jubilee of Queen Victoria.

Without him our town would not be half the success it is, but even Sir Thomas Bennett was overshadowed when the Queen came to town in 1958. He accompanied the royal party through the streets of Crawley, while cheering crowds waved flags for the young monarch.

Sir Thomas was a renowned architect, responsible for much of the development of Crawley and Stevenage. In 1947, Sir Thomas was appointed as the chairman of the Development Corporation of Crawley New Town, a post he held until 1960.

In his early days at the Development Corporation, he was responsible for the scrapping of the existing plans for the new town, and the appointment of Sir Anthony Minoprio to create the town's new master plan. He died on 29 January 1980.

Security for any royal visit is high, but when the Queen was in Crawley on 9 June 1958 she could not have been safer with the Guard of Honour of the 275th Field Artillery RA 'Q' Battery to watch her back.

She was accompanied on the inspection by Captain D.P.S. Terry.

Her Majesty and Prince Philip were then greeted at the Territorial Army Centre by Lt Colonel G.T. Birch, commanding officer of the 275th Field Artillery RA. On the left is the Duke of Norfolk.

The children of Three Bridges Junior School were on their best behaviour as they lined up to meet the Queen and Prince Philip (below). Jenny Ramsay was one of the children. She said, 'I am in the group of children in the front row near the Queen's shoulder. I was also in a parade of Brownies who met her in front of the George Hotel, but I do not have a photograph of this.'

Miss Rae Carman, 75, is the daughter of Hepzibah Carman, who was chairman of the council (then Crawley Urban District Council) in 1958. Miss Carman said, 'My mother was in a group of people who were presented to the Queen in the High Street. Several people went up and curtseyed. She went into the George to have a meal with the Queen.

Picture credit: Jenny Ramsay

'I worked in the High Street in Willicks' Stationers where Barclays is now on the corner, but I had time off from work to watch the Queen.'

The picture right was taken in Queens Square in 1958 and shows a team of the Crawley great and good being presented to Her Majesty.

It shows, from the left: Ernie Stanford, Reg Tridgell, Henry Brooke, Alf Pegler, Nellie Simpkins, Dick Barry, Eric Vygus, Bert Crane, Ray Dawson, Ted Lynch, Bert Lumley and Bert Crane (senior).

The picture right was taken in the council chamber in the town hall in 1969 just after the Conservatives had taken control of the council. It shows, from the left: Bert Crane, Elsie Fowler, Roy Davis, Eddie Wignall, John Young, Bob May (after whom a Tilgate school was named), Ted Lynch and Bert Lumley.

Queen Elizabeth has visited Crawley on three occasions: on 9 June 1958, 17 December 1969 and on 3 November 2006, with one earlier visit in 1950 as Princess Elizabeth.

The new town has blossomed over the decades and the changes since her visit to open Holy Trinity School in Gossops Green, in 1969, presented a very different town as it celebrated its 60th birthday.

Accompanied by the Duke of Edinburgh, the Queen visited the recently rebuilt Thomas Bennett

Community College and stopped off at County Mall and Queens Square – where she once planted a tree. The royal party listened to a music group and viewed students' work at Thomas Bennett.

One of the most obvious changes to the town centre since the Queen's previous visit was the building of County Mall. Her Majesty's visit to the mall included a stop-off at Druckers Café to meet local business representatives.

Back problems forced the Queen to leave the Duke of Edinburgh to carry out a visit to the Carey House sheltered housing scheme and Varian Medical Systems.

THE QUEEN MOTHER

The Queen Mother laid the foundation stone of St Catherine's Hospice. The much-loved royal matriarch came to Crawley in November 1982 and was greeted by Mayor Alf Pegler and given a tour of the half-finished Malthouse Road Hospice.

As these pictures from the *Observer* archive show, she was given a warm welcome by the people of Crawley, who turned out in numbers to greet the nation's favourite great-gran.

The first patient was admitted to the hospice in 1983 and it was formally opened in 1984 by the Duchess of Kent.

DIANA, PRINCESS OF WALES

The patients at St Catherine's Hospice were given a surprise to remember when Diana, Princess of Wales, paid them a visit in 1988. The Princess stopped by on 29 August and cheered up a drizzly day for staff and patients at the Malthouse Road Hospice with her trademark smile and hands-on approach.

Greeted by the vice-Lord Lieutenant of Sussex – and the usual cheering crowd – the Princess chatted with patients and cut a cake that was decorated with the hospice logo.

A visit from the Princess is one of those events that you never forget – and one group of schoolchildren will always remember the day they met the lady in question.

David Manuel remembers it clearly. He said, 'In 1988, I was the headteacher of Southgate West Middle School. As we had visited the hospice on occasions to sing carols to the patients, I was invited to bring a few pupils to meet the Princess. We waited outside for a quite a while – well-behaved of course!

'Then Princess Diana appeared and approached me with a coy look on her face saying, "I hope you haven't been waiting too long." The pupils were delighted that they had met her.'

SPORTS

THREE BRIDGES FOOTBALL CLUB

The sporty bunch from Three Bridges Football Club grinning for the camera are proudly showing off hard-earned silverware from the RUR Cup in 1982–83.

Margaret Brown's son Christopher is kneeling at the front of the shot. Mrs Brown, of Broadfield, said 'He was the Three Bridges FC mascot and this picture was taken after they won the RUR Cup in about 1982–83. The white-haired gentleman just behind my son [fifth from left] is my dad, Raymond Fiddes, who was the steward of the club for several years, running the bar and the tea bar – serving burgers and hotdogs to spectators and players!

'In fact, when Three Bridges had a bad fire, my dad was called in by the police and he stayed there all night guarding the stock.'

Mr Fiddles eventually left the club due to health problems. He died in 2003.

Sitting next to Mr Fiddles is Doug Oliver (to the right) and next to him is former club chairman Jim Steele. Mrs Brown added, 'The footballer in the centre behind my dad is Bobby Nash, who was a very popular player, captain and friend. He did an awful lot with youngsters in football and was a great loss when he died suddenly.

'The man on the end of row two [first right] is Alan Knight, the manager then, and the young man on the first right is Gavin, who was the groundsman and kept the pitch immaculate. I used to help my dad behind the bar on match days.'

Tom Wadley is pictured sitting in the front row, second from the right. His son Colin Wadley, of Furnace Green, said 'He was on the committee at Three Bridges FC for a number of years in the early 1980s. He went to all of the matches, and helped organise behind the scenes on match days and many of the social events run by the club. He was very involved with the club at this time and took great enjoyment and satisfaction from his efforts.'

Jean Steele, chairman of 4th Worth Scouts, said 'As far as I know, fourth from the left in the back row is Bill Norris, first on the left in the middle row is Harry Easton, fifth is Bobby Nash and last is Alan Knight. The front row, third from the left, is Paul Terry, next Alan Ladd, then Ray Fiddas, Doug Oliver, Jim Steele, Alf Blackler, unknown, and finally Gavin Currie.'

JOINT CRAWLEY SCHOOLS FOOTBALL TEAM

Horse-racing fans may claim to follow the sport of kings, but the rest of us know that football should hold that title!

In 1935–36, these serious-looking lads were the best schoolboys in the county, having won the Sussex Cup. The team was the Joint Crawley Schools Football Team – believed to be the first joint schools team to represent Crawley.

Picture credit: Peter Cheesmur

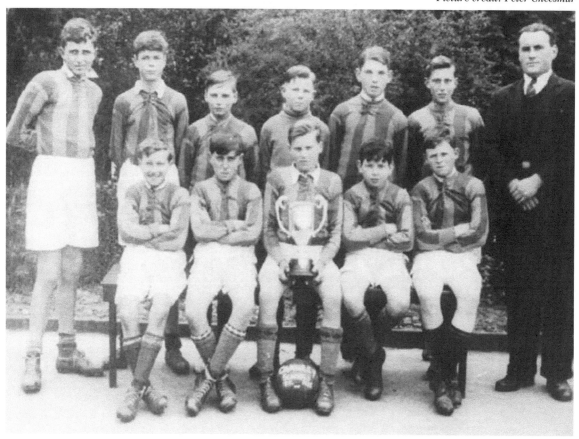

The picture belongs to Peter Cheesmur, whose father, Roy, is standing in the back row, second from the right. Also in the picture is Harry 'Diver' Bacon, on the bottom row seated on the far right. Mr Cheesmur said 'Some of these boys went on to be prominent business personalities in and around the Crawley, Ifield and Three Bridges areas.'

He said the team was formed by the teacher Mr Mansell Jones, an ex-rugby player from Wales. 'It was formed out of the two schools in Crawley at the time – the council and the church.'

Tom and Ivy Foster.
Picture credit: Lesley Hunt

Lesley Hunt, of Ontario, Canada, said 'The young goalkeeper was my dad, Tom Foster, who was 13 years old at the time. Dad loved soccer all his life and took me to games right from birth (so I'm told!). He went on to play for Three Bridges, Horsham and then professionally for a short time for Brighton & Hove. Unfortunately, he couldn't afford to take the time off to attend midweek training sessions, as this was in the days when there was almost no pay for playing professionally.

'Tom served in the Royal Air Force during World War Two, and while stationed in Scotland played for a season (I believe) for Stranraer. After the war years Dad went to work for James Longley & Co., and he remained with them until retirement. He began as a humble painter and worked his way up to site manager, taking charge of some large jobs for the company, such as the shuttle link between the terminals at Gatwick Airport and Sussex University.

'Sadly, Dad passed away late in 2004, after 61 years of marriage to Mum, Ivy Foster, who continues to live in Langley Green.'

THE RAMBLERS CRICKET TEAM

Like most good ideas, the Ramblers cricket team was conceived in a pub.

It was a Saturday night in 1947 and a group of friends was shooting the breeze over a pint or two in the White Hart when Shiner Wilson suggested forming a team. Eddie Thomas, of Southgate, was one of the original members. He said, 'Twenty-four of us saved half a crown a week for 12 months and we started the Ramblers. The team included Sid "Shiner" Wilson, Les Hall, Philip Bastable, Alan Penny, George Barker, Fred Kennard, Eddie Thomas and another Sid [whose last name Mr Thomas cannot recall]. The players paid two shillings in subs for every game and soon built up a following.

Mr Thomas said, 'Two old boys used to follow the team. They used to walk right across the pitch at noon and be ready with their pints.'

STONES FC

You can keep your Premiership with its £80,000-a-week pay packets – if you want to know what football's all about just head to the park on Saturday afternoon.

Stones FC is believed to be the oldest-running Saturday league team in Crawley, and in 2007 the club celebrated its 50th anniversary. Manager Barry Edwards started as a player in 1981 and managed the team from the early 1980s, still pulling on his boots to play a game or two in the 21st century.

Stones, who were also known as Stone Platt and Stone International, were playing as Stones Sports when they became Premier Division Champions in 1957–58. Later, the club had three teams competing in the league. They won the Junior Charity Cup in 1976, the Senior Cup in 1986 and the Junior Cup in 1984. They won the Third Division in 2004 and the Junior Shield in 2004–07.

Barry said 'We have also won the Sportsmanship Award five times and Club Secretary Award in 1993 with a few more honours – 50 years and we're still going strong. I could not have done this all on my own – you need help. We have a great secretary and treasurer in Gary Jones, who runs a tight ship.'

Picture credit: Barry Edwards

CRAWLEY ATHLETIC FOOTBALL CLUB

The picture overleaf belongs to J. Cheal, of Broadfield, and shows the players of Crawley Athletic Football Club in 1928–29.

The victorious lads had just won the Horsham and District League Division Three. Mrs Cheal's father, Harold Pattenden, is sitting at the front on the right. She said, 'When we took the picture out to scan it, his wedding picture was behind it!'

The definitive footballing man, Harold ran the line in his later years, but Mrs Cheal said he also enjoyed a bit of cricket.

Picture credit: J Cheal

The other people in the picture are: back row (left to right): H.J. Briggs, E. Carmen (treasurer), A. Hilder, S.L. Izard, A.J. Miles, J. Simes (vice-captain), E.J. Pellen (hon. secretary), W.A. Draper and D. Collison (trainer). Middle row: H.G. Briggs, C. Elliott, A.Whalley, H. Broomfield (captain), F. Hedger. Front row: F. Elliott, H. Pattenden.

NTC FOOTBALL TEAM

This bunch of likely lads are the members of the NTC football team from the early 1960s. The pictures belong to Julie Fiveash, of Southgate, and the bottom one shows her future husband, Graham, grinning for the camera on the front row, second from left.

The team had just beaten Portsmouth 2–0 away before a crowd of 200 people. Mrs Fiveash says the picture was taken between 1960 and 1963. Crawley Town fans may be interested to note that general manager Barry Munn is in the picture, along with his father.

The team were: Standing from left: Winters (left wing), Evans (centre-forward), Dystkin (inside-left), Rod Warner (goalkeeper), B. Munn (right wing), R. Lucas (right-half), Canliff (centre-half). Kneeling, from left: Dunster (left-half), Graham Fiveash (right-back), Perkins (left-back), Coleshill (inside-right), Horwood (reserve). The manager, Mr Hill, is standing on the left and the trainer, Mr Munn, is on the right.

Football was not the only skill this talented bunch could turn their hands to. Julie said, 'Apparently the NTC [Nautical Training Corps] was situated in an old house or mill behind the Royal Oak pub in Ifield. The boys helped to renovate it and made the inside resemble a ship. We are not sure if it is still there.'

Picture credit: Julie Fiveash

Picture credit: Julie Fiveash

CRAWLEY RUGBY CLUB

This line-up shows the men of the 1927–28 Crawley Rugby Club team, but the only name on the picture is that of team captain, S.R. Matthews.

The picture graces the wall at the Rugby Club and has raised a question or two. Vice-president Ted Smith said, 'Our present club dates from 1950, but this picture is much earlier. Was there a Crawley team continuously between the two world wars? If so, where did they meet and, more importantly, where did they play and whom did they play?'

Picture credit: Crawley Rugby Club

THREE BRIDGES V SUSSEX, 1958

Many fine players have stepped up to the wicket in Three Bridges over the years, but in 1958 a true legend came to town. This picture shows the players who took part in the Three Bridges v Sussex match and belongs to Peter Allen, of Three Bridges.

Batsman Ted Dexter is standing under the clock. Ted was captain of Sussex from 1960–65 and became England captain in 1961–62. He played 62 Tests, scored 4,502 runs and had an average of 47.89.

Picture credit: Peter Allen

CRAWLEY TOWN FOOTBALL CLUB

Whether they support Manchester United or Crawley Town, football folk are cut from the same cloth – dedication and enthusiasm all the way.

The players of Crawley Town FC have been sending their fans to giddy heights and depressing lows for well over a century and, as these pictures show, some stalwart names have been with the club for years.

Picture credit: Crawley Town Facebook

These young gents made up the team of 1968–69, who won promotion to the Southern League Premier Division, though the team did not stay there long.

Former player, manager and chairman John Maggs is on the back row, fourth from the left, while Dave Haining is on the front row, second from the left.

Reds boss John Maggs certainly got a soaking at the end of the 1983–84 season (below left) and with good reason! Crawley had just made their return to the Premiership – a position they held for 20 years until the double-winning 2003–04 season, which saw them promoted to the Conference.

This picture below right shows the team of 1956–57. Former manager and goalkeeper Stan Markham is in the back row, sixth from the left.

Crawley were originally founded in 1896 but re-formed twice, in 1935 and 1938. The club's first game after the 1938 re-formation was on 3 September 1938. They lost 3–2 to Brighton North End.

Crawley played five seasons in the West Sussex League before entering the Mid-Sussex League. They won the Senior Division in their second season.

After playing in an Emergency County League competition in 1945–46, the club stepped up from junior football to enter the Sussex County League in 1951.

Picture credit: Crawley Town Facebook

Picture credit: Crawley Town Facebook

After four seasons in the First Division and one in the Second, Crawley moved to the Metropolitan League, a competition for professional and amateur sides. Retaining their amateur status, Crawley won the Metropolitan League Challenge Cup in 1959. The club turned professional in 1962 and joined the Southern League in 1963.

For the next 20 years they played in the First Division, apart from a brief taste of Premier Division football in 1969–70.

In May 1997, the last ball was kicked at Crawley Town's Town Mead home. The club had been playing football at the ground for 48 seasons, but change was in the air as the magnificent Broadfield Stadium became the team's new home.

The Town Mead ground was sold for redevelopment and the land is now part of Crawley Leisure Park.

The first match at Broadfield Stadium was a friendly against First Division Port Vale on 24 July 1997. The stadium was officially opened by the Minister for Sport, Tony Banks MP, on 19 October 1997.

The top picture shows the aftermath of the FA Cup game against Barnet in 1993 when a wall collapsed.

Below it is the boardroom box, which offered a fantastic view of the Town Mead ground from on top of the stand.

Being a die-hard football fan has never come cheap. The programmes for sale at today's Crawley Town games are glossy, full-colour affairs complete with pictures of the team, ground and staff and will set you back a few quid.

This programme from 1949 was much more basic and cost the princely sum of threepence, though if the printing number in the top-right corner is anything to go by, attendance was much higher back then! The adverts for local businesses were much simpler as well. Note the phone numbers: Crawley 100 or Crawley 28 for the best fish in town!

This programme was from the 1979–80 season and was a bit special. Current club vice-president Jim Green used to work at ITN and approached Glen Miller, one of the ITN graphic designers, to design this cover. There was no charge made to the club. Glen now owns his own graphic design company.

The Crawley Town trophy cupboard may sometimes be a little bare, but the club has earned its fair share of silverware over the decades.

The Sussex Professional Cup took pride of place at Town Mead in 1970, the Gilbert Rice Floodlight Cup in 1980 and 1984, the Southern Counties Combination Floodlight Cup in 1986, and the Sussex Senior Cup in 1990 and 1991. The Sussex Floodlight Cup was won in 1991, 1992 and 1993.

Picture credit: Crawley Town Facebook

Arguably the club's finest moment came in 1991–92 (below) when Crawley Town reached the FA Cup third round proper and the town went down with a severe case of Cup fever. The run was ended by Football League neighbours Brighton & Hove Albion at the Goldstone Ground in front of 18,301 fans, but Crawley had defeated Third Division Northampton Town at home 4–2 in the first round to get there.

This team pulled on the red shirts in the 1977–78 season and includes: Alan Poecock, Vic Bragg, Martin Chilvers, John Leedham, Ricky Fitzgerald, John Maggs, Wayne Peacock, Dave Easton, Tony Mulhern, Ali West, Brian Roberts and Dave Haining.

The team of 1991, who had every reason to celebrate after winning the Sussex Senior Cup.

Overleaf we have the team of 1960–61 – the Crawley side who hold the dubious honour of conceding the most goals in one season – 123. The biggest surprise must be that, considering they finished second bottom, there was a worse team in their division! The players include Fred Cunnell and Stan March.

Picture credit: Crawley Town Facebook

Do you remember when FA Cup fever took a hold of the town? Where were you when Crawley kicked League side Northampton Town out of the Cup with a 4–2 thumping?

In 1991, Steve Hedges, Nigel Betteridge and John Rowell were spurring the Reds on to victory with

Picture credit: Crawley Town Facebook

their song *Come On You Red Devils*. As inspirational songs go, it certainly did the trick, and the team made it to the third round proper of the Cup – a feat they have never been able to repeat – beating Northampton on 16 November and brushing aside Hayes on 7 December with a 2–0 away win.

The dream run ended on 4 January 1992 when, with Northampton's scalp under their belts, the players travelled to the Goldstone Ground to face First Division neighbours Brighton & Hove Albion – one of only four non-League teams to make it that far.

They lost 5–0 in front of a 18,301-strong crowd, earning the club a very nice cash boost.

Crawley boys Steve, Nigel and John made up the group One Touch To Go and they composed *Come On You Red Devils* in September 1991. Steve was on drums, Nigel on keyboards and vocals and

Picture credit: Crawley Town Facebook

Picture credit: Crawley Town Facebook

John was on bass. Steve said, 'We were known for our original rock music (we wrote most of our own material) and we were at our live performance peak from about 1986 to 1993. When the arrival of our children slowed down our live work we retreated into our own studio.

'The Red Devils tune was to help promote the Crawley Town FA Cup run and was one of the first projects we created in the studio. Aimed at being a contemporary pop tune (rather than a Chas and Dave style cliché), it was used on Radio Mercury and BBC Radio Sussex in interviews and as an intro to their Crawley Town FC reports at that time. It was also played over the Crawley Town PA system. A limited edition of the song was released on cassette, with the B side being one of our One Touch To Go original compositions.'

The success of the Crawley Town song saw the band asked to do the same for Football League club Brentford FC. They produced 1,000 cassettes and their music was regularly played over the Brentford PA system to crowds of 6,000. Steve said 'As often happens, the band gradually drifted apart, as John left for Wales and work commitments prevented regular get-togethers.

'But not before One Touch To Go had produced a trio of albums which, while never really selling in great numbers, were well received by their small but loyal fanbase. Nigel is currently working with local band the Noodleheads and his son is now following in Dad's footsteps as the driving force behind top local band Us and Them.

'Myself, I am still involved with recording projects.'

Perhaps a song is just what today's Reds need to help them to a successful Cup run!

THE WAR YEARS

VIOLET MEADUS

Wartime throws up heroes in many guises, from the ordinary men and women determined to do their bit, to the brave souls on the front line fighting to protect their countrymen.

Violet Meadus was newly married and not long out of her teens when she witnessed an act of heroism that saved her life. Violet and her sister, Olive, worked for R. Cook and Sons Ltd, the builders on the junction of West Street and Oak Road.

It was July 1944 and Germany had developed a frightening new weapon, the Vergeltungswaffe-1, or V-1, known in England as the flying bomb, buzz bomb or doodlebug. On 10 July a doodlebug came down on Crawley, despite the best efforts of one heroic Spitfire pilot.

Olive died in November 2006, but in 2007 Violet, of Turners Hill, still had vivid memories of the events leading up to the devastation that left seven people dead and 44 injured. She said, 'We'd just checked in after lunch break but I didn't go right to my bench. The sirens went off at the top of Goffs Hill. No one took any notice. I kept walking. I went out but I didn't run. It wasn't frightening. I looked up and there was this Spitfire. I thought "whatever's that man trying to do?" Then the flame (at the back of the bomb) stopped and I thought "my God, it's coming down" and I rushed back in and screeched "get out, it's coming down".

'Cook's built houses before the war. I went out and laid down in a pile of sand and that's all I remember. I couldn't get up and it was like you

were eating dust. Some one moved and then there was this hand. Then I saw a face and I thought "that's Elsie". She worked opposite me.

'I said "Elsie?" She said "yes" and I said "what's the time, darling?" It was 3.15pm. We had been unconscious for three hours.

'Elsie lived in Copthorne. Her father was a stretcher bearer. I said "you'll be late for your bus". I walked to the bus with her and from there I'm blank. I don't know how I got home. My mother grabbed me and cried and cried and cried. My hair was on end and I was all cut in different places. I said later that the Spitfire pilot was a brave man going so close. He was trying to prod (the bomb) up into the field. You heard all sorts of heroic things they did. He came to the site later to see Mr Cook.

'It all happened in seconds really. If it had come straight down it would have been curtains for me, but it came down in front of the building in Oak Road. The flame stopped and it fell.'

While many would have hidden themselves away, desperate to stay safe, Violet and her friends were made of sterner stuff. When her boss, Leslie Cook, appealed for help clearing the bomb damage from his factory, she went back for what proved to be the last time. She said, 'I went back one day and it was the first I had seen of the carnage. I walked on the debris where the office would have been and I found this thing. It was a hard crust and some string. One of the demolition men shouted "that's a scalp" – what a thing to say. I dropped it and I never went back again. It sounds cowardly but I have never been up there again.'

Although she was never to work for Cook's again, Violet recalled small details of her time there as if it were yesterday.

While the firm built houses before the war, it was requisitioned for wartime activity and, in particular, the workers made fuel tanks for Spitfires. She said, 'I think about 150 people worked there.

I had to weld this thing that went up into the wing and when I had done that it went through the door into the shop. Gladys had to put a skin all over the wing and then spray it. She smoked like a chimney! She was meant to drink two pints of milk a day but she used to take it home for her two children.'

Violet married her sweetheart, Reg, in 1943: 'A lot of us did – we knew D-Day was coming.'

Like so many young war brides, she soon had to wave her brave husband off to war and a time of terrifying uncertainty.

Speaking highly of her boss, Mr Cook, a gent who was not usually one to show his feelings, she remembered one time that he proved to be a great comfort: 'One time, I was working and I was leaning on my bench and there were tears and I felt a hand on my back and it was Mr Cook. He said "he'll be alright".'

The factory was run by Leslie and his brother Don, who had a house in Springfield Road. Don died not long after the war.

Violet said: 'I think Mr Cook died of cancer. He had two daughters, Jennifer and Josie.'

With her place of work destroyed, Violet went to work helping deal with bomb damage around the town. 'Talk about suddenly you're a plumber!' she laughed.

Violet's job was to carry out distempering work on damaged homes and she described one particular act of kindness that has stayed with her over the years: 'One day some dear little old lady was walking along the street and said "my dear, do you do distempering?" She said "mine wasn't bombed, but I'm old and I need my sitting room distempered". We asked the foreman – he was a good one – and he came back with two cans of distemper. We said "that will come out of our wages" but he said "no" and he let us have it for free.'

One point Crawley history buffs will find interesting is the fact that the old lady's house was 'opposite the old laundry' where the infamous 'Acid Bath Murderer', John George Haigh, conducted his grisly business.

Violet and Reg had many happy years together after the war. They had two daughters, Lyn and Anne, and Violet dotes on her three grandsons – one of whom was named after his grandfather – and one granddaughter who became a vet in London.

Reg died in 1995 and Violet's nephew John Oliver became a regular visitor at his aunt's Turners Hill home. He said, 'Reg came over with the Canadian forces during the war – as did my father. After the war Reg was responsible for a lot of the clearance work necessary to build Crawley New Town, and there is a picture or two of him in books of local history. One thing is for sure, the war had quite an impact on

Crawley, even apart from the bombs. Violet and her two sisters Olive (my mother) and Ivy all married soldiers stationed there from across the UK and Canada.

'During the war our family (they were called Humphries) lived at a house on Horsham Road which has passed on to me following mum's death. The house is in a time warp – it has hardly changed at all since those days. But Crawley itself has, of course, changed beyond recognition!'

Mrs Meadus's account of the day a doodlebug destroyed Cook's stirred family memories for Sharon Ottley. She said, 'My grandfather, Leslie Bevis, was a driver for Cook's and with his job came the bungalow he lived in with my grandmother Rose and nine of their 11 children at 55 Newlands Road.

'In 1944 Lil, their eldest, was married and lived in Brighton. Bill was serving in the Navy, Len worked at Teetgens in the High Street, Bob worked for Cook's also, Joan worked at Woolworths, Gwen (my mum), Ivy, Charlie, Ethnee and Edna were at school and Val, the youngest, was a baby.

'When the doodlebug was heard, Bob luckily ran out the back of the yard – he would have been killed had he gone to the front. The bungalow was flattened along with the house next door and five houses opposite.

'Mrs Ayling died in the house next door and also her daughter Mrs Startup, who lived in the next house along.

'Rose, Ivy and Val were at home and, fortunately, a beam had fallen across a bed and protected them from certain death. Len ran home from the High Street to find Bob digging them from the rubble that had completely buried Val and injured the others. Luckily they all survived. They lost everything in the bombing and the family were then split into small groups and taken in by friends and relatives. All of them have different stories to tell and those that are still around today remain very close.'

It is hard for anyone born after World War Two to imagine what it is like to be bombed out of your home and workplace.

One member of the Denman family was in her mother's house in West Street when the bomb fell, while her mother, Sarah, and sister, Winnie, were working in Cook's factory when it was hit. She said, 'My mother lived in West Street about 100 yards from where the bomb fell. The house was badly damaged and was later demolished. They managed to get some things out but we pretty much lost everything. It was pretty horrible. I was in the house. I got a very bad cut on my leg.

'My eldest sister had a baby two days later. She lived in Oak Road and bricks went through the pram that they had bought for the baby.'

The family – including her younger brothers, Frank, Sid and John – went to live with relations until the council rehoused them. She later moved to Deerswood Road when the houses were built. Our lady was unlucky to even be in town when the doodlebug fell. Serving in the Land Army for five years, she was on leave having had an accident at work. She said, 'We did all the farm work. It was hard work. For the first month I wished I was dead but once you had turned 18 you had to do something.'

Speaking of the bombing, she said: 'The war was the most important thing. You didn't care what was in the house as long as you had your health.

'The worst thing that happened is that someone looted the damaged homes that night. We didn't have very much but someone looted it. The next night they put the Home Guard up there.'

GEORGE HUMPHRIES

Violet Meadus was not the only member of her family to have a close call with a doodlebug. Her brother,

George Humphries, proved to have a guardian angel when a day's work almost ended in tragedy. Violet said 'He was in Ifield ploughing the field with two horses and the first doodlebug fell into the field. If it wasn't for the horses he would be dead. They took all the shrapnel and were cut to pieces.'

A farmer by trade, George used cart horses for his work and could ride with the best of them. He is pictured winning a cart horse derby in Horsham.

Gordon Rice, of Langley Green, remembered talented horseman George as 'a bit of a lad'. He said, 'He used to have stables on the site opposite Cheal's nursery. When I came home on leave from the Navy he asked me to help with haymaking.

'A bloke called Jim "Jasper" Lee used to run the farm. In 1949 he gave me the sack when I took the day off to go for a medical in Brighton. I went anyway and when I came back he gave me two of the worst jobs. I had to go all the way up to Milton Mount to cut thistles. On the Saturday he fired me. He even charged me for half a dozen eggs for my mother!'

Mr Rice said Mr Lee used to farm Gossops Green, Southgate, and down to the Mill Pond. He is believed to have moved to Lingfield after the council bought his land.

The doodlebug strikes on Crawley during World War Two are still very clear in the memories of many of the town's older residents, especially those who were only children at the time of the attacks.

Nadine Hygate provided information from the records kept by the Home Guard about three 'flying bombs' that fell within the jurisdiction of Crawley and Ifield Parish Council. One also fell in Poles Lane, but that was considered Lowfield Heath.

The first fell on 30 June 1944 in Ifield in a field at the end of the common, near a school and church.

The second was the 10 July bomb in Oak Road. Seven people were killed and 44 injured. Fifteen houses were demolished.

The third fell on 2 August 1944 in allotments to the rear of Malthouse Road. It came down in the middle of the night but did not explode. The houses were evacuated and the Ministry of Defence removed the bomb, which was the first in the country to not explode.

Miss Hygate's account of the 10 July bombing reads: 'At the time of this event our family were staying at my grandfather's home in Station Road. Since my grandmother's death the previous year we alternated with our own home in Ifield Road on a monthly basis. On this particular day, a Tuesday, Cook's the builders were replastering two bedroom ceilings badly cracked in the previous year's bombing. They had just finished when the doodlebug exploded and brought down all the new plaster!

'My grandfather was walking through the level crossing by the railway station. The next he remembered was finding himself some way down the High Street in a shop doorway, where the blast had blown him.

'For myself, I was at school. I was educated at Crawley C of E School, which was located at the corner of Victoria and Ifield Road. Since the destruction of the infants' building, which fronted onto Spencers Road, during the previous year's bombs, all pupils over 11 years attended the Council School.

'The infants, with Mrs Stobbart, were given room in the main school building. My classroom was a wooden structure in the centre of the playground, and lessons were under the tuition of Miss Davies and the headmaster, Mr Weston.

'We had air raid shelters, but I do not recall using them, except for many practice drills in the early stages of the war. Also at this period we were not carrying our gas masks. When the siren sounded, if you were able to reach home within five minutes, then you were allowed home, but were required to return upon the "all clear".

'Flying bombs made a terrible noise, and when the engine stopped you knew it would glide down and explode. As children we watched them during the day, only taking cover after the engine stopped. From the sounding of the alert until the bomb exploded was only a few minutes in this incident.

'My job was to collect my brother, who was in the infants' department, and go home. All the infants had been seated on the floor in the internal corridor, which had no windows. My brother refused to come, and at that moment the engine stopped and the bomb exploded. All the infants screamed. I pulled my brother out by his hair and ran!

'As we went round to the corner towards the High Street, we were met by a wave of people running toward the school, who thought that was where the bomb had fallen. They stopped and asked me. On reaching Ifield Road corner we met my grandfather coming to find us.

'Entering the High Street, we were confronted by a picture which forever remains in my memory. There were shops at that time in the upper square. The roads and pavements were covered with glass. Every single shop in the street had had its windows blown out. My school had not, and schooling continued as usual.

'As an adult reflecting on the incident, if we had left school immediately, as we should have, my brother and I would have been in the High Street when the bomb exploded.'

Gordon Rice also has clear memories of the day the V1 doodlebug destroyed Cook's factory. He said, 'We had just moved out of the row of houses that was destroyed. We lived at number 18 and it wiped out all that row of houses. Also Mr Pollard's wheelwright yard on the far side.'

His sister-in-law Lily worked at Cook's and lived with her mum and dad in Oak Road. He said, 'Her son, Brian, was sitting in his high chair in the garden when the doodlebug hit. He was completely covered in dust. He lives in Saltdean with his wife and kids now.'

Roger Barnard is a lucky man. Although too young to remember the events of the doodlebug strike on Oak Road, he had a close call when it fell. He said, 'My mother tells the story of the doodlebug that fell in Oak Road, like Rex Williams, at first hand. I was there too, but too young to remember.

'My mother was pushing me, aged eight weeks, in the pram along Springfield Road when the doodlebug cut out and came down just the other side of the row of houses. She had pushed me from home in what is now Goffs Lane and was on her way to the clinic in the old Congregational Church in Robinson Road.

'Of course, she was not aware of where the bomb would land, so bent herself over me in the pram and waited. She stayed bent over the pram until the debris and dust had subsided, before walking quickly on to the clinic, both of us thankfully unharmed.

'At the baby clinic, our doctor, Dr Ronnie Matthews, was gathering his team together to go to the bomb scene, everyone having heard the explosion close by, and so, of course, the clinic was cancelled. My mother turned round and went home. She was met by my grandmother, living with us at home, who had also heard the explosion and hurried in the direction of the clinic along the same route. All returned home safely. However, when picking me out of the pram my mother noticed "a small shiny piece of metal" lodged between the mattress and the side of the pram. This was a piece of shrapnel from the doodlebug itself. My mother and I were both very lucky.'

DOODLEBUG WINGS

They may look like bits of scrap metal, but these pictures show the remains of a doodlebug tail. The piece was loaned by Rex Williams and gives a fascinating glimpse into the workmanship of the flying bombs.

The top picture shows faded German text, while the one beneath still shows the blue paint, which was used to camouflage the craft against the sky.

In his book *You Must Remember This*, Mr Williams, 73, has documented his memories of some of the doodlebug incidents in Crawley. Regarding the bomb which failed to explode in Malthouse Road, he said, 'The doodlebugs were supposed to dive when the engine cut, but this one belly flopped to the ground. I remember that one fell at night. The motor must have cut out. I suppose it ran out of fuel.'

He was waiting to enter the Scout hut in Goffs Close when another flew right overhead on its way to Springfield Road alongside the railway line. After the explosion at Oak Road, he and some other lads ran to the site to volunteer their services, but were told that they were not required. He was lucky enough to witness the efforts of an Allied pilot to divert another bomb. He said, 'I was standing behind the Embassy (now Bar Med) in the field. A whistle blew and a flare went up then the doodlebug flew over. A Hawker Tempest arrived and put its wing under the doodlebug and tipped it up. Because it was a Tempest it was almost certainly a Polish pilot from West Malling.

Picture credit: Rex Williams

'I dived into a ditch and put my hands over my ears. I took my hands off just when it exploded in Poles Lane, Lowfield Heath. When I took my hands away I saw I was next to an ammunition shed.'

The bombs were even more frightening when you couldn't see them as they passed over. My brother and I were walking in a field that is near Ewhurst Road. There was thick fog. It was a bit alarming because we couldn't see anything.'

The bomb that came down on Ifield Green was passing over Mr Williams's house when the engine cut. He said, 'We were in the garden and watched it come over. The engine cut out over our house. We went into the kitchen and hid under the table. It came down in Ifield Green and blew a man over a haystack.'

While the idea of Crawley being targeted by bombers is terrifying, Mr Williams summed up the versatility of children when he said, 'At first we were quite excited but after a while we didn't even bother to look up.'

Mr Williams used to work as a builder's surveyor for Longleys.

One of Rex Williams's most vivid memories of wartime was the day a Tomahawk single-engine, single-seat, low-wing, all-metal fighter and ground attack aircraft made an unscheduled stop in Crawley. He said, 'Late one morning, when at school in Crawley, news arrived that a Tomahawk P40, as used by John Wayne in *The Flying Tigers*, had crashed at Ifield.

'We always went home for dinner and this was about a mile each way. Seeing the crash would make it two miles each way, so we had to get moving.

'As we arrived at Ifield we could see the crash had occurred about 50 yards past the Royal Oak pub next to Telmey's Garage (later Berite Motor Factors).

'The single-seater fighter, flying from west to east, had followed the direction of Rectory Lane, hit a tree and telegraph pole and sliced through the top of each on the Post Office side of the road. Part of the tailplane was in the tree. It had then crossed the road with the fuselage going through the 12ft-wide gap between No.2 Alma Cottages and No.1 Oak Cottages.

'The pilot neatly left one wing on each of the tiled roofs. As the fuselage was at the far end of the gardens in a greenhouse we were not allowed to see more. We heard the pilot sprained his ankle. The tree with no top was felled in 1987 at the time of the hurricane.'

With Allied soldiers from all over the world stationed in Crawley, it was only natural that the local girls would find themselves the centre of attention. Parents in Crawley did not always approve. Mr Williams recalled, 'If Johnny, the handsome young Canadian soldier who visited our home to call on my 17-year-old sister, had had the sense to call himself Horace or something, my parents might have allowed him back again.

'My other sister had a boyfriend for a while called Cliff, from Bradford. He told me VR on his RAF uniform stood for "very reluctant" and also suggested a very rude cure for my chilblains. I can't repeat what it was but it had something to do with emergency night-time toilet arrangements, considering our urinal was outdoors. He gave me an altimeter from a crashed Junkers 88 for my collection.'

Another old Crawley man with clear wartime memories is Mr Hilder, from Littlehampton. He has clear memories of the doodlebug which, despite the efforts of one brave pilot to use his own plane to nudge it away from danger, fell on Cook's in 1944. He said, 'I was born in Crawley and was a telegram boy during the war when the Post Office was hit. I was about 16. I started work in 1942.'

While others have said the plane which tried to divert the flying bomb was a Spitfire, Mr Hilder disagrees. He said, 'It was a Tempest because Spitfires were too slow. We heard it come towards us and that cannon fire had a shot at it. Then the Tempest tipped its wing and it came spiralling down. The Post Office was in Grand Parade, having been bombed out in 1943. We just got flat on the ground because we thought it was coming down on us.'

Mr Hilder lived in Malthouse Road at the time and spent all his working life with the Post Office.

14TH AFV (ARMOURED FIGHTING VEHICLES)

Crawley may have been only a small village during World War Two, but the young men and women of the time certainly did their bit. In 1943 Eddie Thomas was 18 and stationed with the 14th AFV (armoured fighting vehicles) in Old Horsham Road. Mr Thomas, of Southgate, said the AFV was one of several units based in Crawley, including the REME (The Royal Electrical and Mechanical Engineers), ATS (Auxiliary Territorial Service) and RALC (Régiment d'artillerie légère du Canada). He said, 'The women were at the Mount in Rusper Road. Our barracks was opposite St Wilfrid's School and the headquarters were in a big house on Goffs Park Road – Hillplace. The southbound carriageway on the roundabout was completely blocked for traffic because of the tanks coming in.

Picture credit: Eddie Thomas

'There was an inspection pit for the tanks and lorries and we would make them serviceable for the soldiers. We would get a convoy of them and take them around the south of England and camouflage them so they were there and ready for use.

'I was taught how to drive a tank on Salisbury Plain. They came back here and were unloaded and we made them ready for service. They were loaded onto trains at Three Bridges Station. We used to have little gun carriages and we used to race to Three Bridges. They used to go at about 35mph.'

During the war, Crawley was home to huge numbers of Canadian soldiers and, naturally enough, not all their stories had a happy ending. Mr Thomas said, 'I was told to take the three-tonne Bedford to pick up 11 Canadian soldiers from Tilgate Forest and take them to Aldershot Barracks. I was told not to pass too many pubs as they were special. First stop was the Dog and Duck in Horsham at opening time! We arrived in Aldershot at tea time – 5 or 6 o'clock. Weeks later we heard that not one soldier returned from their tank. We never heard why that was.'

Mr Thomas was one of four brothers who went to war and was stationed in Germany for two years when the fighting ended. He met his wife Mavis at the Congregational Church in Robinson Road during the war where she was helping her mum prepare teas for one of the concerts that was held there.

Picture credit: Eddie Thomas

Mrs Thomas witnessed a pilot's attempts to tip the wing of one of the doodlebugs which eventually fell on the town. That night she headed out. She said, 'I went to the Old Punch Bowl. My mum was disgusted that we went out when people had died.'

Mr Thomas was in the cinema when the bomb fell. He said, 'Plaster fell from the ceiling. We went back to the barracks to help.'

Mrs Thomas also remembered the 'stick of bombs' that demolished the old Post Office and chuckled at one lighter moment amid the uncertainty of the war: 'I can remember being in the dining room and my dad heard the bomb and said "duck" and my mum said "yes dear?"'

HEATHER PESKETT

Like many young women during World War Two, Heather Peskett took up the challenge of working the fields in the Women's Land Army. But while most returned to their old lives once the war ended and the men came home, Heather enjoyed her work so much that she stayed. She joined up on 14 August 1942 and this is her story.

Picture credit: Heather Peskett

'I was born in Crawley, and have lived here all of my life. When I left school at 16 years old, I went to work for Mr Norris who owned Tilgate Forest Lodge, Pease Pottage. I cycled to and from work, seven days a week.

'For the first six months I was involved with the harvest, then I began working with cattle, which required feeding and watering daily. I joined the Land Army when I was 17 and was allowed to stay with my employer, Mr Norris, instead of being sent elsewhere. When the Land Army was disbanded in 1950, I was happy to stay on. When I started work at the farm there were eight Land Girls and 14 men and boys. When I retired, the same farm of 800 acres was worked by five people!

'Harvest was very hard work as there were no combine-harvesters. The corn was cut by binder. There were three tractors...very modern for those days, as most farmers in this area still used horses. We had to stand the sheaves up in blocks of six. If they fell down we had to start again. These were left standing for two weeks at least, and then they were loaded onto carts and taken to the rickyard, where they were built into ricks.

'In mid-winter, the contractor steam engines came to thresh the corn. By this time I was working with the bullocks, which were

being fattened for market. This meant grinding mangolds and swedes in a machine similar to a mangle, which was worked by hand. The ground vegetables fell in piles onto the floor, to be mixed with rolled oats or barley and linseed cattle-cake, and this was distributed twice daily around the mangers.

'Hay was put into the racks and had to be cut out in slabs, and straw was renewed for bedding.

'In the spring the cattle went into the fields, and they and the fences were checked every day. Then there was the hoeing! Acres and acres of swedes, mangolds and sugar beet.

'After about a year of this, one of the girls left and I took over her job of hand-milking four Guernsey cows and making butter and cream. Also, 30 pigs as well as the bullocks. No spare time in the winter! In summer the cowsheds and buildings were whitewashed and creosoted.

'After the war Mr Norris started a dairy herd, beginning with Ayrshires, but eventually changed to breeding Friesians. I did not specifically work with them, but had the calves from about two months old, through their life. The steers sold at 18 months, and the heifers until they calved at 30 months and went into the herd. At the same time I looked after the bulls.

'By this time we also had a herd of pedigree Wessex Saddleback pigs (black with a white stripe across the shoulders), which were my charges. This I greatly enjoyed. Pigs are greatly maligned I think – they are great fun. At the peak of my work I was responsible for (with minimal help for extra jobs like worming, warble fly dressing, TT testing) four milkers, 100 young stock and about 100 pigs.

'A 50-hour week was often the minimum. My starting wage was £1 1s 11d [£1.10] per week, and in 1974 was the grand sum of £17.44!

'After the war more machinery was invented and available to the farmer, which made the outside work easier, but was little help to the animal keepers. However, it cut down the number of workers needed, which gradually became less as men died or retired.

'The young men realised that other occupations gave them more money and free time, and somehow the family feeling went as the tractor drivers were alone for most of the day. But, even being wet through, cold, or sweltering hot, I enjoyed it all immensely and have many happy memories of people and events.

'It has been calculated that in the first 40 years I cycled 100,000 miles to and from work, and I continued to work for a further four years.

'In 1983 I received a Long Service award at the South of England Show, for 40 years of service on the same farm.'

Picture credit: Heather Peskett

Heather's grandfather was Alfred Peskett, who built a lot of houses around the older areas of Southgate. When she was five, she moved into one of the houses he built and has lived there ever since.

One night during World War Two, a doodlebug fell into the allotments behind the house – but did not explode. Heather believes it to be the first one in the country that failed to go off. She said, 'The police came and moved us out. We were moved in with friends. We took the dog and left the cat. I had to go to work. I just came back here, got my sandwiches and went.'

While some people may find the idea of living in one house for virtually your entire life strange, Heather is completely happy where she is: 'I never thought of moving. The family were well known. My dad (Jack) was on the parish council.'

Like so many 'old Crawley' people, Heather was educated at the Robinson Road School before going on to Horsham High School. Of her teachers, she remembers Miss Bennett, Mr Reeson, Mr Groves (the headteacher) and Mrs Walpole (who was then Miss Harris). She said, 'There are a few people from those days still around that you see now and then – Eddie and Mavis Thomas and Jean Avery. You kept to your own area really. Three Bridges was almost a foreign village!'

Heather has seen a lot of changes in Crawley over the decades and said: 'We had a lot more useful shops. There were six good grocers in the High Street. Now everyone is expected to have a car.'

Heather retired at 60 after 44 years. In 2008 she was presented with a medal for her services as a Land Girl by Prime Minister Gordon Brown.

SID BEARD, TILGATE FOREST LODGE ESTATE

Sid Beard was manager of the Tilgate Forest Lodge Estate in 1947. He said, 'I have known Heather since that time as a worker and as a friend, which she remains to this day. Heather was a great worker, cycling out to the farm in all weathers.

'It was only when the snow was too deep to cycle that I picked her up in the Land Rover. She was a dedicated worker who loved her work and the

Picture credit: Sam Beard

cattle she tended from weaning until their entry into the dairy herd or when they were sold.

'She was fearless in handling cattle as in those early days there was no handling equipment, health and safety legislation was unknown and as a result one was often subjected to knocks and bruises. Heather had her fair share, but was never put off by such assaults. She, like many other girls, did a man-sized job, diligently and well.'

CRAWLEY HOME GUARD

With World War Two finally at an end, the men of the town's Home Guard took to the High Street for their victory parade. Among them was Raymond Chantler.

He may not have been young enough to get the call to fight for King and country abroad during World War Two, but Frank Withers was determined to do his bit.

Picture credit: Colin Edgar

His daughter, Stella, said, 'He lived in Crawley from 1914 up until he died in 1982 aged 82. His brothers Sid, Ted and Bill all lived in Crawley, as did his sisters Dolly and Edith; although Edith did emigrate to Canada after the war. In 2007 she was the only one still alive at 92.

'I can always remember seeing him in his uniform and tin hat when I was a child, during the war. When the sirens used to go, he always rushed out to make sure everyone was safe and sound around where we lived in Woolborough Road, and in surrounding roads in Northgate.

'He also used to drive the Greenline buses up to London. He used to tell us stories of the terrible bombings and suffering he used to see on his journeys.

'I am not too sure which is Dad in the picture but he is definitely there somewhere – it's difficult to recognise the ones at the back.'

THREE BRIDGES HOME GUARD

Mention the Home Guard and most people think of *Dad's Army*, but there was nothing bungling or inept about these men. This picture belongs to Pete Allen, of Three Bridges, and shows the volunteers of the Three Bridges Home Guard.

Picture credit: Peter Allen

The Home Guard website (*www.homeguard.org.uk/hg/history*) states: 'The Home Guard was formed when there was a real risk of invasion. Most men who could fight were already in the forces, those that were left were either too young, too old, or in reserved occupations (those jobs vital to the war effort). The men who volunteered to join the Home Guard at this time were expected to fight an invasion of crack German troops with nothing more than a collection of old shotguns and pieces of gas pipe with bayonets welded on the end!

'The Government was expecting 150,000 men to volunteer for the Home Guard. Within the first month, 750,000 men had volunteered, and by the end of June 1940, the total number of volunteers was over one million. The number of men in the Home Guard did not fall below one million until they were stood down in December 1944. The Home Guard was disbanded on 31 December 1945.'

The men in this picture include, front row from left: Fred Russell, Bill Setford, unknown, Harry Jordan, unknown. Back row from left, Frank Denman, Dennis Russell, unknown, unknown, 'Ranji' Horn, unknown, unknown.

THREE BRIDGES HOME GUARD AND FIELD MARSHAL MONTGOMERY

This picture was snapped during World War Two and features some of the men of the Three Bridges Home Guard at Three Bridges Station as they gathered round a distinguished VIP.

The guest – his chest adorned with medals – was none other than Field Marshal Montgomery, who was ferrying his staff round all the Home Guard HQs in the country.

Picture credit: John Sumner

The picture belongs to John Sumner, of Langley Green.

As well as doing his duty for King and country, Mr Sumner's father, Hector McDonald Sumner, was a steam engine driver based at Three Bridges. Originally from Cheshire, Hector was living in Hazelwick Road at the time and his sons, John and Derek, were born at that address. He died of a blood clot in 1954 at the age of 54 when John was just eight years old.

Picture credit: John Sumner

IFIELD HOME GUARD

This picture of the men of the Ifield Home Guard belongs to Joseph Burchell, of Northgate, and was taken outside the Plough Inn, near the church, during World War Two.

Mr Burchell was a lad of just 16 or 17 years at the time. He

Picture credit: Joseph Burchell

said, 'I wasn't allowed to have a rifle because I was too young so I was the platoon runner. I would take messages everywhere.'

Mr Burchell, who left school at 14 to work as a builder, named Lt Wilson as the platoon officer-in-charge and also remembered John Flint, Sgt Parsons and Mr Ellis.

When he turned 18, Mr Burchell joined up, training with the Royal Sussex Regiment before serving abroad with the 7th and 9th Royal Scots and the Argyle and Southern Highlanders.

BALCOMBE VICTORY HALL

This picture belongs to Rex Williams, of Turners Hill, and was taken outside the Balcombe Victory Hall, which was built in memory of those who died in time of war.

Picture credit: Rex Williams

WAR CHILDREN

Standing to attention as well as any soldier, this young lad and his sister were unveiling a dedication to those who fell in battle.

The picture of the pair, who lost their father during World War Two, was taken by the *Crawley Observer* photographer in the early 1950s.

The plaque still adorns the entrance to the Memorial Gardens.

WORK

1950S STRIKE MARCH

When you think of mass protests you tend to think of the 1960s. But Crawley proved to be ahead of the times when the workers took to the streets in the 1950s to protest at a council-imposed rent rise.

These pictures belong to Tony Syrett, of Pound Hill, whose brother worked for Edwards High Vacuum at the time and was involved in the march.

Mr Syrett, who paid a 26-shilling rent on his house when he moved to Crawley, said, 'The strike march started in Manor Royal and all the factories were involved.'

Picture credit: Tony Syrett

Picture credit: Tony Syrett

Picture credit: Tony Syrett

CRAWLEY AUXILIARY FIRE BRIGADE

The men of Crawley Auxiliary Fire Brigade at the old fire station in Ifield Road. The man on the far left is Edwin Godsmark.

Picture credit: Marion Godsmark

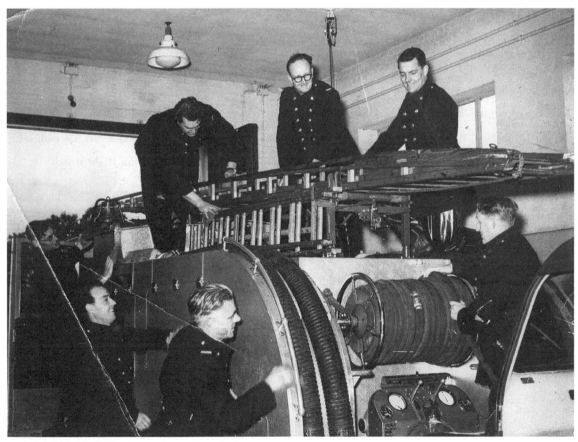

Picture credit: Shelia White

WORKS OUTING

This picture belongs to Sheila White, of Langley Green, and shows a group of colleagues from either Crawley Metals or Bell Machines on a boat in Southend during a works outing.

Mrs White's husband, Derek, is in the back row, third from left. She said, 'He was about 18 in the picture. He left the Robinson Road school at 14. He was one of the last 14-year-olds to leave. We met in 1952.'

CRAWLEY METALS, CHRISTMAS 1947

Office Christmas parties have certainly changed over the years. Gatecrash a festive bash today and dickie bows and party frocks will be few and far between. Not so in the 1940s.

This happy bunch worked for Crawley Metals and were snapped celebrating Christmas in 1947. The picture belongs to Malcolm Elliott, of West Green. Malcolm's dad, Percy, worked for the company, which Malcolm said was sited where the extension to Southern Counties stands, on Ifield Road.

Picture credit: Malcolm Elliott

Malcolm said Shirley Thomas, who lives in Langley Green, is one of the women in the picture.

Former Crawley Metals worker Stella Slight, from Horley, was able to put a few names to faces in the Christmas party photograph. She recognised her sister Daphne Gugolka (neé Withers) who died in April 2007; Daphne's husband Stanley, who stayed in England after the war; her mum Ivy Withers who died in 1998; Ivy who lived in Ifield Road; Mr Mundell, the managing director of Crawley Metal Productions; Mr Mundell's wife; two Italian sisters whose names she cannot recall, one of the Beavis sisters and Mr Rose.

'In fact I went to work there in the offices of Crawley Metal Productions directly I left school in July 1954 and stayed there until January 1958.

'Ivy, Mr Bird, Mr Rose, Mr Mundell and one or two of the others still worked there when I did. The lady standing next to my mother in the picture also worked there with me but I cannot remember her name.

'Others I remember in my time there are Sue Elliott, Edie Whalley, Rosie Mulvaney, Bob Foster, Les Joyce, the telephonist, Norman in the drawing office, Mr Bartlett in the accounts office and a guy called Ginger who worked in the packaging department which was situated opposite in Victoria Road. Also Michael Barnard, who was one of the office managers and always insisted us juniors called him "sir". Mr Rose used to frighten the life out of me as he was always so stern. Many a time I used to be in trouble for sitting talking to the telephonist in the front office, which really was no more than a cubby hole, but you could hide behind the door.

'When I started work I was earning £3 5s a week and my wages went up to £3 15s before I left.

'Summer holidays were always the last week in July and the first week in August – the whole factory closed down then, that was the only holiday you got. We used to get a bonus for the holiday which for me usually worked out about £13 or £14 – I used to think it was a fortune and used to rush out to buy clothes in the new Rosina Boutique that had opened in the Broadwalk.

CRAWLEY AIRCRAFT PRECISION TOOL COMPANY

This picture shows a group of workers gathered outside the Crawley Aircraft Precision Tool Company, which stood in Tushmore Lane, at the site later taken over by Metal Box.

It belongs to Malcolm Elliott, who said, 'Dad worked for them but he is not in the picture. Those are all the high-up people.' These hard-working men and women had their noses to the grindstone with the country embroiled in the beginning of World War Two.

The remaining pictures belong to Rex Robinson, of Pound Hill, and show the workforce of the Crawley Aircraft and Precision Tool Company in 1940. The

Picture credit: Malcolm Elliott

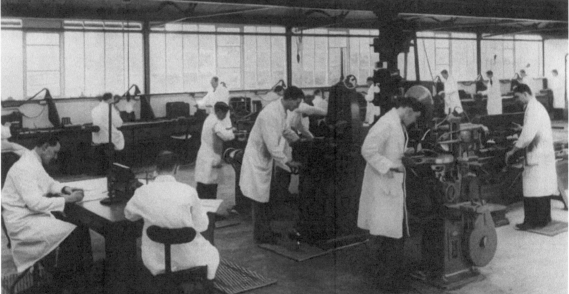

firm was based on London Road and Rex, who has lived in Crawley since 1937, is pictured in the group shot. He is second from the left on the front row and was a working man at the tender age of 14 years nine months.

It was not all work, work, work at the Crawley Aircraft and Precision Tool Company in the 1940s.

This picture shows everyone dressed to the nines and is labelled 'Pat's party, 21st, November 18 1944, Empire Hall, Horley'. It looks like a good time was had by all.

STONE-CHANCE IN THE 1950S

Picture credit: William Godfrey

Of all the products that spring to mind when you think of Crawley, lighthouses are unlikely to be high up the list – but for the workers at Stone-Chance in the 1950s they were a major part of the job.

These pictures belong to William Godfrey, of Langley Green, who used to work for the Manor Royal-based firm.

Mr Godfrey, 81, moved to Crawley from Sutton in 1953 to set up home in the new town and became part of a team whose skill and brains in crafting lighthouses and beacons helped ensure the safety of pilots and sailors across the world.

This picture shows senior lighthouse fitter Len Seddon working on the optic of a lighthouse destined for South Africa – one of 30 he hand-built during his 42 years with the company.

Next is the biggest lighthouse lantern built by Stone-Chance. Measuring 10ft 6in in diameter, it was eventually sent to India.

Picture credit: William Godfrey

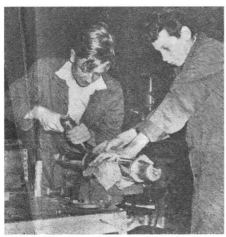

Picture credit: William Godfrey

Picture credit: William Godfrey

These lads are general engineering apprentices Raymond Payne and David Saunders working on a Sumo Pump, while next is Joe Whitehouse, watching one of his assistants working on a telecommunications station.

Then we have David Gibbons, checking the fog detector which stood on the roof of the Stone-Chance building, while B. Durden is tackling the complicated job of rewiring a control cubicle.

Picture credit: William Godfrey

Picture credit: William Godfrey

They say that the best friends are old friends, and former Stone-Chance employees Dave Saunders and Ray Payne have known each other for a very long time. Dave and his wife Wendy moved to East Grinstead while Ray called Pease Pottage home.

Wendy hails from Three Bridges originally and met the two boys when they moved down from London to the new town. Dave was a pupil at Ifield Grammar School while Ray went to Hazelwick.

Engineer Dave stayed at Stone-Chance for about a year before pursuing his career in engineering, while Ray went on to own an engineering firm.

BALE AND CHURCH

The birth of the new town saw an influx of companies setting up home on the newly-built Manor Royal – and one of the first to arrive was Bale and Church.

These pictures were sent in by Julie Fiveash, whose dad, Tony Leader-Chew, moved to Crawley with the firm from London in the 1950s.

John Bale's late great uncle A.E. Bale, Ernest Wrench, Beryl Newman and his late father, R.J.J. Bale.

Picture credit: Julie Fiveash

Tony Leader-Chew and two unknown men packing tins of Kleenoff.   *Picture credit: Julie Fiveash*

Keen to learn more about her father's place of work – which used to make Kleenoff oven cleaner – Mrs Fiveash got in touch with John Bale, whose father ran the company. Mr Bale was able to fill in a few gaps and said, 'Bale and Church moved to Crawley in 1952, I believe in November of that year. Prior to moving to Crawley, Bale and Church had operated from a 400sq ft factory on the fourth floor of a building in St Mary Axe in the City of London.

'Bale and Church brought with it to Crawley at least three members of staff – Jo Chapple, Albert Ladd and Tony Leader-Chew.

'Bale and Church remained in Crawley until 1990 when the brand Kleenoff was sold to Jeyes of Thetford. The factory ran for

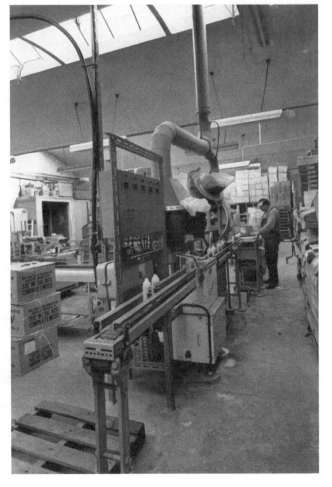

Tony Leader-Chew packing Kay Dee Kettle descaler some time in the early 1960s, probably 1962.
Picture credit: Julie Fiveash

This photograph was taken in the early 1960s and shows a group packing Kleenoff Squeeze Bottle refills. The middle lady on the left side is Olive Champion.
                                            Picture credit: Julie Fiveash

The general office with Beryl Newman, Stella (last name unknown) and two unknown women.

                                            Picture credit: Julie Fiveash

Picture credit: Val Ward

another year and the subsidiary company Woodall, Bale and Co. Ltd continued to operate for another 15 months or so before being wound up. Bale and Church was the second factory to be opened on the Industrial Estate, APV being the first.'

Mr Bale recognised most of the people in Mrs Fiveash's pictures. He added: 'The Kleenoff brand is still about but, due to changes in legislation, one will only find it in a small number of hardware stores. The major supermarkets do not stock the brand as it is a slow-moving item.'

Tony Leader-Chew died 10 years ago.

Val Ward, from Broadfield, has fond memories of her years at Bale and Church as 'one of the girls'. She said, 'I worked for Bale and Church, the Kleenoff Company, in approximately 1954–55. What fun times and how lovely working for a small family concern.

'I remember Beryl Newman well. She was the secretary of the company and looked after us girls in the office. I remember Tony Leader-Chew also. He was a nice man, a real gentleman. Mr A.E. Bale died when I was there and I also remember Mr John Bale – a good boss to us. Mr Ernest Wrench was always called "Sir Wrench"! I also remember Albert Ladd and Jo Chapple.

'The girls in the office when I worked there were Stella Waite (moved to Crawley Down), Gail Burningham (moved to Canada), Pat Horton (moved to Horsham), a young girl called Carole whose surname I forget and me, who was then Valerie Stammers. We worked hard but also had loads of fun there and the atmosphere was quite relaxed. I learnt a lot of typing and book-keeping skills when I worked at Bale amd Church.

'The typewriter Beryl Newman is sitting at is a Royal and it is the very typewriter I used too. Beryl used to telephone me when she wasn't coming into the office and dictate letters to me via the telephone (I was a fast typist!).'

SUGG'S

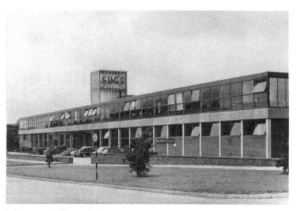

The birth of the new town saw a massive influx of industry and Crawley became home to firms such as APV and Stone-Chance.

One of the biggest companies to come to Crawley was Sugg's, which set up shop in 1955. Founded by William Sugg in 1837, Sugg's had a long and successful history in the gas industry before coming to Sussex. After a takeover in 1969, a group of former employees started a new company in 1973, which became Sugg Lighting Ltd – which is still in business on Gatwick Road.

This picture of the Sugg premises holds painful memories for Janet Sheehan. Janet, whose maiden name was Roberts, worked for the firm before she married. She said, 'I remember working for Sugg's in the typing pool in 1965–66. I was 21, had a birthday party at home at the weekend and went to work as usual on Monday.

'While sitting typing, I noticed a rash all over me. The supervisor sent me home and I went to the doctor's and he said I had German Measles. So I will always remember my 21st!'

CRAWLEY FIRE BRIGADE IN 1934

Their engine may be a little small and their ladder a little rickety-looking compared to those used by today's firefighters, but this fine crew looked just as suave in their uniforms.

This picture shows the men of Crawley Fire Brigade in 1934. Fred Martin's father, Fred Snr, is in the picture.

Mr Martin Snr finished his career as chief officer and Mr Martin Jnr still has the clock with which he was presented when he retired at 65. Mr Martin named: Sid Stanford, Fred Martin, Bert Miles 'who died quite young', Bart Ockerton, Charlie Bowers and Charlie Cooper.

Mr Martin believes the father of one of the firefighters was the verger at West Crawley Church and

he knows that one of the firefighters was also a butcher. He said, 'The station was down Ifield Road, just before you went into the George. They had two engines when I was a boy. They had a Dennis and a Ford. They used to go out in the engine and, if there was room, they would take me.

'Dr Ronnie Matthews was the chief officer at the time and if he

Picture credit: Peter Allen

went along then I couldn't go. So I didn't like him much when that happened!'

Here are two sets of heroic lads from the 1940s. The picture above shows the men of the Three Bridges Auxiliary Fire Brigade in 1941 with firefighter Jim Laker kneeling at the front.

The second photograph shows Crawley Fire Brigade in the 1940s. The firefighters include Mr Mitchell, Mr Miles, Mr Pavey and Mr Skinner, while the third photograph shows a view of the old

Picture credit: Peter Allen

Crawley Fire Station in Ifield Road – a far cry from today's station! We have no idea who the gent in the foreground is.

LONDON TRANSPORT SNOOKER TEAM

This cutting belongs to former mayor Brian Quinn and was taken from the *Crawley and District Observer* of 3 May 1968. It shows the Crawley bus drivers who made up the London Transport snooker team who won the third division of the Horsham and District Snooker League at the first attempt. The victory earned the team promotion to division two, at intermediate level.

The cutting read: 'The team was presented with the divisional cup at Roffey Sports and Social Club, and each player got a set of cutlery.'

The men in the picture are, from left: Fred Millward, Harry Lockey, Frank Whelan (captain), Brian Quinn, Charles Smith, Sidney Bell (secretary) and Norman Miles.

Brian says that Sidney Bell is now living in Australia.

LLOYDS REGISTRY OF SHIPPING

When enemy fire damaged the Lloyds Registry of Shipping premises in Southwark in April 1941, it set in motion a string of events that would see the firm move to Crawley in the 1950s. After the war, with part of the firm's premises beyond repair, visits were paid to Stevenage, Harlow and Crawley and, in 1951, Lloyds took out a 99-year lease on a site in Manor Royal.

There was snow on the ground when the first turf was cut by the printing house manager on 6 January 1953 and on 16 May 1953, a commemoration stone, placed near the main entrance, was laid by Lady Garrett. The building is known as Garrett House.

These pictures were provided by Brian Mitchell, of Southgate, whose father trained as a printer with the firm. Information provided by Mr Mitchell read: 'By August 1953, it was possible to transfer the composing room, reading room, monotype and intertype departments to Crawley, where they were able to embark on their first big task.

Picture credit: Brian Mitchell

Brian Mitchell's father in training.
Picture credit: Brian Mitchell

Picture credit: Brian Mitchell

Picture credit: Brian Mitchell

'Completion of the machine room and warehouse rapidly followed, and by the end of 1953 the whole of the printing department was installed and in operation. The posting department followed in February 1954, and by the end of February the administrative department of the printing house had taken over their quarters. Including the administrative department, the printing house staff consisted of some 120 persons. By the summer of 1954 the research laboratory was completed and in occupation.'

GARRETT HOUSE

There is more to printing than meets the eye if these pictures are anything to go by.

Bill Cox, who worked as a printer's assistant at Garrett House, publishing the *Lloyds Register of Shipping*, was full of information about life outside the office.

Mr Cox started work at Garrett House in 1955 and stayed for 11 years. He moved to Crawley with his wife Trudy and his baby daughter after eight months of commuting from Dagenham. He said the Crawley branch of Lloyds closed about 20 years ago, moving to Burgess Hill. He described his working environment in the machine room as 'an antiquated sort of affair' and described how he would have to make any alterations to the print by hand.

Speaking about his old workmates, he particularly recalled Fred Stansbury, who worked for the printing firm his entire working life – the only time he missed being his service in the Navy.

The staff's out-of-work activities included cricket, football and table tennis – the latter included a league stint 'with a certain amount of success'. The cricketers played matches against teams from other Manor Royal factories and the line up included: Tom Brewer, Alan Pullen, Mr Wingrove, Ray Young, Bill Skinner, Alan Love and Vic Cobbett.

Picture credit: Bill Cox

As well as being a decent cricketer, Ray Young was a dynamic right-winger and played football for Crawley Town, while Mr Cox turned out for Ifield cricket team as a bowler.

As far as football went, 'when you played for Lloyds you played wherever you could'. The line up included: Vic Cobbett, Ron Davis, John Kemp, Mr Stubbington, Ted Rowell, Ray Young and John Skinner. Ted Rowell went on to become manger of the printing office.

Mr Cox says the works outing was organised by the staff and was probably to Margate. The picture includes: Mr McCullam (with the accordion), George Duncalfe, Vic Cobbett, Bill Cox, Fred Skinner, Bill Brinkley, Fred Stansbury, Alan Love, Bob McLean, Fred Elson and Glenn Gafney.

Mr Cox described such outings as 'wayzgoose', which is 'a holiday or party for the benefit of printers, traditionally held in August'. (It is also an old English term for a fat goose suitable for stuffing!)

Picture credit: Bill Cox

ND - #0136 - 270225 - C0 - 276/195/12 - PB - 9781780914008 - Gloss Lamination